New Pathfinder 6
Lights, camera, action!: Digital video in the languages classroom

New Pathfinder 6
Lights, camera, action!: Digital video in the languages classroom

Ruth Bailey and Claire Dugard

CiLT The National Centre for Languages

New Pathfinder 6 – *Lights, camera, action!: Digital video in the languages classroom* first published 2007 by:
CILT, the National Centre for Languages
20 Bedfordbury
London WC2N 4LB

www.cilt.org.uk

ISBN-13 978-1-904243-63-2

A catalogue record for this book is available from the British Library

Printed in Great Britain by Hobbs the Printers Ltd.

CILT Publications are available from Central Books, 99 Wallis Rd, London E9 5LN. Tel: 0845 458 9910 Fax: 0845 458 991. Web: **www.centralbooks.com**

Acknowledgements

This book has come about thanks to a small but very important number of people, who gave us so much inspiration and support in different ways. A very special thank you must go to:

- BBC 21st Century Classroom Centre staff and Steven Fawkes
- Cathy Chicksand and Sally-Ann Tomkins, Shireland Language College
- CILT colleagues Christopher Amugen, Terry Cooper, Ann Swarbrick and Richard Winston
- Alan Crease, Royal Grammar School
- Ian King, Brookvale High School
- Mark Pentleton, Partners in Excellence
- Alex Savage, Notre Dame High School

We would also like to thank the teachers and pupils of all our project schools for all their ideas, enthusiasm and persistence!:

Aylesbury High School, Aylesbury; Belle Vue Girls' School, Bradford; Brookvale High School, Leicester; Coombe Girls' School, New Malden; Cotswold School, Bourton-on-Water; Elizabeth Garrett Anderson High School, London; Ian Ramsey CE School, Stockton-on-Tees; Kings Norton Girls' School, Birmingham; Miltoncross School, Portsmouth; Moseley School, Birmingham; Notre Dame High School, Norwich; Prince Henry's Grammar School, Otley; Purbrook Park School, Waterlooville; Queen Mary's High School, Walsall; Royal Grammar School, High Wycombe; Shireland Language College and Shireland City Learning Centre, Smethwick; South Wolds School, Keyworth; St Julie's Catholic High School, Liverpool; The Holt School, Wokingham; Tile Hill Wood School, Coventry; Torquay Boys' Grammar School, Torquay; Wirral Grammar School for Girls, Bebington.

Finally, we would like to thank our CILT GTP trainees and CILT colleagues, who helped us to translate film-making terminology into French, German and Spanish:

Emeline Galibert, Chalin Malz, Katya Möller and Gabriela Porter, Laura Rafael Redondo and Jose Luis Torres Sánchez, Birgit Stoberock and Natasha Ricot-Gómez.

» Contents

» Introduction

Storyboarding, filming, capturing, editing – these are not terms heard as a matter of course in the languages classroom. Surely film-making with pupils is a bit too complicated and technical to be part of teaching languages? This point of view was close to our own, but as the potential of **digital video** (DV) technology in other curriculum subjects was highlighted repeatedly from the late 1990s onwards, we were intrigued as to the impact it could have on language teaching and learning. After all, surely film-making and language learning share the same aim of effective communication? Clearly there would be opportunities for concentrated oral practice and a sense of a real audience. Working in more varied ways with video might also benefit a wide range of pupils through its appeal to visual, auditory and kinaesthetic learning styles.

As language teachers, we have a long-established relationship with the medium of video. We play foreign language films, programmes and advertisements recorded from TV, and language learning videos to our pupils. We now benefit from the additional features offered to us by DVD. Some of us take video footage on trips abroad to bring the target language culture into the classroom. Others video pupils in class for assessment purposes or to celebrate achievement. We might have done much more in creating our own video, but **VHS** had its limitations. Recording equipment was often cumbersome and expensive, the visual quality of footage was relatively poor and recordings on tape were difficult to edit, with only a few basic effects and titling options available. Opportunities for dissemination were limited by the need to haul a TV and video player into the classroom to play even the briefest clip, and the difficulties of copying footage onto tape to share with colleagues and pupils.

Digital video makes all the difference. It is completely possible to be spontaneous in lessons with **point and shoot** activities, as we call them in this book, thanks to cameras that are small, light, easy-to-use and relatively cheap. Footage is better quality and there is less pressure on how you film thanks to the wide range of editing options available. Editing software is easy-to-use and very often free. Footage can be played on a laptop or desktop computer and viewed through a data projector and on an interactive whiteboard. It is easy for teachers to distribute multiple copies of recordings to pupils or to incorporate clips into teaching resources without loss of quality. This is not to suggest that digital video production is problem-free, however, far from it! Our and our colleagues' experience has highlighted not only the kind of things that can go wrong, but also the fact that most problems are surmountable.

DV made simple

Digital video
The capturing, manipulation and storage of video using a digital format. Digital video can be transferred to a computer to be edited and then delivered in a variety of different formats, with no loss of quality.

VHS (Video Home System)
This is an analogue, non-digital video format.

Point and shoot
Originally used to describe easy-to-use cameras with a minimum of controls, we use this term to refer to the simple acts of turning the video camera on, aiming it at the subject and pressing the record button.

Meeting Mark Pentleton of Partners in Excellence early in 2003 was the final push we needed to set about exploring the possibilities for languages of this new improved medium of digital video. His team had been running film-making weekends for post-16 students learning languages across Argyll and Bute, and East and North Ayrshire in western Scotland with highly impressive results. We decided to explore the possibilities for extending the scope of this work in two key directions: firstly, taking digital video work into the school classroom; and, secondly, working with younger people, namely KS3 and 4 pupils (ages 11–16). The key to progress and success was clearly going to be the involvement of the language teachers, so the Digital Video in the MFL Classroom research and development project was conceived.

The Digital Video in the MFL Classroom project

CILT, the National Centre for Languages, set up the Digital Video in the MFL Classroom project in collaboration with the BBC 21st Century Classroom (21CC) centre in 2004. With the aim of supporting pupils making films as part of their language learning, two teachers from each of twelve secondary schools in England designated as Specialist Language Colleges came to London for a two-day conference. They spent one day at CILT exploring ideas for language projects and one day at the BBC 21CC centre, learning technical skills through the creation of their own one-minute film. They then went back into schools to develop their ideas and, with support from CILT, to set up language-focused projects with pupils. The teachers all met again in London several months later to showcase project outcomes and share problems and solutions. The project, known as the CILT/BBC 21CC project ran again in 2005–06 with a second cohort of language teachers.

Participating schools discovered that many (and sometimes unexpected) pupils were keen to perfect and show off their MFL skills in front of the camera, demonstrating renewed levels of confidence and motivation. This book features many examples from the project and from other schools who have also been working in the medium. One school, for example, worked with a local special school to film a rendition of *Ghostbusters* in Spanish. Another worked with their local tourist office to produce video sequences introducing the area to visitors from French, Spanish and German-speaking countries. The development of language skills was not the only benefit noticed through the CILT/BBC 21CC project and others, such as the Becta digital video pilot project (2002) mentioned on p11. Pupils acquired new ICT skills, which they perceived as highly relevant to their everyday lives. Adapting to a new level of autonomy, they had to develop decision-making and group-working skills at all of the planning, filming and editing stages. They were able to exercise their creativity, in terms of dreaming up script scenarios, using the target language, creating costumes and makeshift sets, framing of camera shots and also to improve their acting skills. The world of film-making is said to have its own literacy which challenges pupils and exposes them to whole new ways of thinking.

Digital video work thus has the potential to contribute significantly to the development of the whole child, and clear links can be made with the aspirations of the Secondary National Strategy, particularly with regard to thinking skills and assessment for learning. It also builds on the principles for good teaching and learning outlined in *Excellence and enjoyment: A strategy for primary schools* (DfES 2003). The potential for working with advanced level students or in a vocational context are further areas for exploration – by integrating digital video into coursework or extended project work, for example, or increasing expectations of target language use and student independence.

You can read more about the CILT/BBC 21CC Digital Video in the MFL Classroom project on the Specialist Language Colleges area of the CILT website (**www.cilt.org.uk/languagecolleges/ projects.htm**).

Structure of this book

While most teachers working with digital video are unlikely to have had the intensive training and support offered to participants in the CILT/BBC 21CC project, it is still perfectly possible to aim for pupils to work on their own film-making projects. Much can be done with simple point and shoot skills, and as you progress firstly to basic editing and then to more advanced multimedia editing, more and more creative opportunities open up, both for you and your pupils. While it cannot be a technical manual, we have written this book to support and guide language teachers working at different levels of skill and experience, from using a digital video camera for the first time, through to setting up ambitious projects with pupils.

Throughout the book, as in this introduction, you will come across 'DV made simple' boxes, clarifying the terminology used in the field of digital video.

Chapters 1 and 2 focus on developing basic proficiency with the technology and simple teacher-controlled activities to support language teaching and learning, whether filming pupils or creating resources. Chapter 1 is about getting started, outlining ideas for point and shoot activities, and includes a focus on assessment for learning. It also provides a basic technical background, and guidance on filming techniques and film literacy. Chapter 2 moves on to developing your material, giving ideas and guidance for how you can exploit editing facilities to enhance the simple footage you have recorded, creating a rich source of teaching materials.

Chapters 3 and 4 move from teacher-led activities to more ambitious pupil-centred work. Chapter 3 focuses on planning pupil film-making projects and explores the rationale for handing the reins over to pupils. It outlines different curriculum models and ideas for a language project focus, as well as strategies to prepare pupils for new ways of working and health and safety issues. Finally, Chapter 4 focuses on facilitating pupil-centred working, giving suggestions for structuring a series of lessons and supporting pupils in their planning. The chapter also provides guidance on maximising language-learning opportunities for pupils as they work independently from you, in their script-writing and in the creation of storyboards and shot lists.

Based on lessons learned from the CILT/BBC 21CC project and others, we hope that this book will provide you with lots of ideas for developing the use of digital video within language teaching and learning, as well as a wealth of practical tips to help you in this learning process. Whatever your current level of skills, available equipment or time and energy, there should be something here you can get your teeth into and we hope that you will find it as exciting and enjoyable as we have. Good luck!

Chapter 1
» Getting started with digital video

- What kind of simple pupil-focused activities will support language learning?

- What kind of teaching resources can I create?

- Does digital video have a role in assessment for learning?

- What hardware, software and other equipment do I need?

- What tips can I pick up on filming techniques and locations?

- How can I develop my understanding of the medium of film?

What kind of simple pupil-focused activities will support language learning?

Whatever your level of ICT skills, you can very quickly start to use digital video (DV) effectively. Even the simplest of activities can have significant impact in the classroom and the most basic of video resources can enhance a teaching sequence considerably. The evaluation summary of the Becta digital video pilot, a research study of 50 primary and secondary schools working across the curriculum, concludes that digital video can:

Motivate and engage a wider range of pupils than traditional teaching methods, so providing greater access to the curriculum; [and that]

Auditory, visual and kinaesthetic learning styles are catered for by the multi-faceted nature of the medium itself. Digital video enables learners to access information and assimilate it using auditory and visual stimulation.

(Burn et al 2002)

These findings clearly have relevance to language teaching and learning and are supported by the experiences of teachers taking part in the CILT/BBC 21CC project.

The **zoom**, record and stop buttons are all you need to locate on your video camera to start using it for real in the classroom; see pp24–25 for details. Why not try using the camera at home first, or with colleagues in the staff room, until you are confident in working it? Start off by filming activities you have planned for your lessons anyway. A simple **point and shoot** focus could be to film pupil performance, of a role play, for example. Performance is an opportunity for pupils to give meaning to the language they are speaking. In some instances, teachers use video as a reward, where the best work emerging from a classroom activity is filmed. However, do make sure that parental permission has been secured for filming pupils (see Chapter 3 for further details).

DV made simple

Zoom

Using the zoom lens on a camera to zoom in or out on the subject, usually with a stationary camera. (See also p23)

Point and shoot

Turning the video camera on, aiming it at the subject and pressing the record button.

Trimming

Editing a video clip to remove excess footage at the start and end.

Video provides a permanent and high-status record of pupils' achievement, and its motivating effect can impact positively on the amount of effort pupils put into everyday activities. With the knowledge that their performance is to be permanently recorded, pupils can be encouraged to focus their role play rehearsals:

• to memorise language by heart;
• to concentrate on their pronunciation and clarity;
• to focus on the use of gesture, body language and eye contact;
• to use tone of voice to reflect what they are saying.

A useful tip is to make use of simple props or costumes, where possible, which can help to reduce inhibitions as pupils take on the role of a target language speaker. Pupils can be invited to vote for the best performances, which can then be 'rewarded' in various ways. They can be used as a teaching resource for peer classes or younger pupils to introduce a new topic, for example. The film could also be played as a looped presentation at an Open or Parents' Evening. Nothing more than **trimming** the start and end of the clip is required as follow-up work for this type of material.

South Wolds School took the role play idea a step further with Year 7 classes and combined talking about personal information with research on the target language culture. Pupils chose a famous person from past or present and researched him or her on the Internet. Celebrities ranged from Napoleon to Astérix, from Albert Einstein to Michael Schumacher. Working in small groups, they then wrote an interview script in the target language, using information about their chosen persona. Complete with costumes and props, each group performed their work to the class, which voted on the best six to be filmed. Brookvale High School had the idea of practising the future tense through role play, with a pupil in each group taking the role of a fortune-teller. Such creative approaches to language practice are particularly effective as a focus for filming.

Other ideas for such a learn-by-heart rehearsal and performance approach could include:

• show and tell presentations, for example, with photographs of pets;
• news reading;
• illustrated presentation about 'My town';
• GCSE speaking presentations;
• performance of simple poems written by pupils;
• office-based role play, where pupils focus on body language and etiquette, as well as language.

If you have a partner school in the target language country but do not have video-conferencing facilities, you can enrich email correspondence with the exchange of brief video clips. Content would depend on age and ability, but could range from pupils giving their name, to asking questions or answering those sent in an email, to presenting a topic of personal interest. Larger files can be sent by post on a CD or DVD, or shared via password-protected web space.

Not all activities suitable for filming require repeated rehearsal and preparation, however, and individual pupils can participate in different ways at different times. Pupils might volunteer to undertake a speaking task in front of the class, for example. Standard classroom activities can also be recorded, or you might film individuals or small groups while the rest of the class is working on another task. Again, the focus is on motivating pupils to greater effort and awareness of pronunciation and the range of communication skills. Examples of classroom activities could include:

- presentation of a weather forecast to the class to practise new vocabulary, using the OHP or images on an interactive whiteboard;
- practice of new language by describing how to reach an unknown location for the class to guess, using a large illustrated town plan;
- 'Who am I?' whole-class game, where pupils make statements about 'themselves' according to the name written on the back of a card;
- 'fashion show style' dressing-up activity, where each pupil puts on an item of clothing and describes what they are wearing to camera, using adjectives and agreement where relevant;
- rendition of a language learning song, with a pupil leading from the front with accompanying gestures;
- with a more advanced class, prepared debate, on the benefits of town versus country living, for example.

The material can usefully be reviewed for self-assessment purposes or retained as a record of achievement at a point in time. Some footage will also be appropriate for using with other classes, to model an activity, for example, to motivate or to serve as a teaching resource.

A Year 10 class at Royal Grammar School was focusing on the distinction between different adverbs of possibility in German, through use of the poem *Bestimmt* (see opposite). The teacher made an impromptu decision to film a pupil reading the poem aloud, using tone of voice, body language and gesture to emphasise meaning. This has now become a teaching resource available on the web at **http://atschool.eduweb.co.uk/rgshiwyc/documents/poem/index.htm**.

A poem - read by a Year 10 pupil from the German class

BESTIMMT

Heute abend werde ich es machen
Ganz bestimmt
Wahrscheinlich
Ich werde es wahrscheinlich Heute Abend machen
wahrscheinlich Heute Abend
Ja, wahrscheinlich werde ich es Heute Abend
machen
Oder Morgen
Vielleicht
Vielleicht Morgen
Vielleicht werde ich es Morgen machen
Ja, ich werde es vielleicht Morgen machen
Ganz bestimmt
Entweder Morgen oder Übermorgen
Ja, möglicherweise Übermorgen
Möglicherweise Morgen
Möglicherweise Übermorgen
Entweder Morgen oder Übermorgen
Bestimmt
Oder Freitag

bestimmt	*certainly, definitely*
ganz bestimmt	*absolutely definitely*
wahrscheinlich	*probably*
möglicherweise	*possibly*
entweder ... oder	*either or*
vielleicht	*perhaps*

In time, you may decide to hand over the filming task to pupils. This is a useful strategy if you have a number of pupils who do not want to appear in front of a camera and also frees you up to note judgments on speaking performance during the actual lesson. If a number of cameras are available, pupils can work in pairs or small groups to record one another. This is likely to result in immediate self- or peer-assessment, with pupils rerecording unsatisfactory first performances.

All the point and shoot activities described in these pages can be achieved with the simplest of filming skills and require nothing more than trimming the start and the end of a clip in terms of editing. Another good starting point is to enlist the co-operation of the ICT department or co-ordinator, which can allow for more sophisticated filming and editing work. Find out when pupils work on digital video at your school and consider whether a suitable mini-project could be set up with an appropriate class. Filming and any additional audio recording would take place in language lessons, whereas editing and production would be completed with the ICT teacher.

You can view such a cross-curricular example for German language beginners on the 'Digital alchemy: Using digital video assets across the curriculum' CD from Becta Publications. Ten pupils stand in a group and the word *zehn* (ten) appears on screen; suddenly, one person disappears with a pop and *neun* (nine) appears, and so on (See p10).

Source: Becta Publications, 'Digital alchemy: Using digital video assets across the curriculum'

This activity could be taken a step further, with the addition of target language audio. In the editing suite, pupils would have to listen carefully to select the best quality recording for each German number, listen to the start and end of each word to clip it at the right point and to match the right audio, text and video together in the correct sequence. The final product is a lovely teaching resource. As well as introducing numbers, the video can be paused for questions and answers in the target language, such as 'How many girls are there?' or 'Name the person who disappeared'. There are many more ideas for cross-curricular working and more extensive projects in the second half of this book. You will also find important guidelines on health and safety and pupil protection in Chapter 3.

A final, but very important point, is that some pupils may not want to be filmed. Likewise, some pupils may agree to be filmed, but do not then want the footage to be made public. It is crucial that pupils feel ownership of the use of their image and, while we would seek to encourage participation, we must ultimately respect their wishes. If you intend to ask pupils to take part, consider the following guidelines which will help to build up the necessary trust:

- tell pupils exactly what the video footage will be used for;
- allow them adequate time to prepare properly before filming;
- stick to what has been agreed;
- be sensitive when using the footage – do not pause the video on an embarrassing image of a pupil, for example;

- if you are setting up pairwork, pupils could initially work in groups of three, so a child opting out can concentrate on operating the camera and joining in peer review until he or she is confident enough to appear before the camera.

Another approach tried out at Frank Wise School – a special school that took part in the Becta pilot project – is the use of toys, such as Playmobil characters, in front of the camera, while pupils provide the dialogue from behind the camera. Stop-frame animation, whereby static objects are moved by a tiny amount from one frame to the next, offers a similar solution and is another technology worth exploring.

What kind of teaching resources can I create?

If you prefer not to start filming with pupils yet, why not create some video-based resources yourself for use in lessons. A second Becta research project, focusing on the use of digital video assets in schools, reported that:

> *Pupils respond better to assets that have been produced by their peers than by professional organisations. They also respond well to resources produced by their teachers.*

> (*Evaluation report of the Teaching and Learning with Digital Video Assets Pilot* 2003–2004, Becta p9)

The focus does not need to be highly sophisticated, nor even contain the target language! Consider the appeal of using images of a moving sky to depict different types of weather, for example, rather than traditional flashcards. You could also film mute sequences around school, such as a view of walking down a corridor or footage of pupils in the playground. These can then be used for introducing and practising new language, such as directions, prepositions and locations, and activity verbs.

Be aware that it is very easy to add a **voiceover** to digital video footage. Slowly **panning** across an interesting scene will afford you the opportunity to add a variety of soundtracks at a later point in time, differentiating the resource for different classes. Avoid the temptation to speak as you film: a polished voiceover can be used over the background of natural sound. Contexts which bring together lots of elements from the same topic area may be useful with beginners, such as a fruit and vegetable market stall, or a high street of different shops, a car dealer's forecourt (for colours) or a sports centre featuring different activities. Ideally such filming would be done in the target language country.

If you do want to bring different target language voices into your classroom through your video materials, there are two obvious sources: visiting a target language country and/or working with native speakers. Remember that this type of resource requires more focused planning and preparation, and understanding of how you intend to use the video sequences in your teaching.

Visiting a target language country

If you have a visit abroad planned, there are all kinds of possibilities for recording useful footage, where cultural information as well as language abounds.

- You could film rail passengers stamping their ticket in France, for example. Shop assistants may be happy to perform a transactional role play with you, although you may have to buy something! Remember to ask permission before you film individual people or in commercial property such as shops or railway stations, however.
- Try asking people on the street for brief opinions or information snippets. They may be more willing than you would think to speak to camera in 'vox pop' style.
- If you are meeting native-speaker friends, there are all sorts of possibilities, such as filming an extended discussion, the cooking of a meal or taking a tour of a house.
- You could keep a video diary of your trip, speaking to camera at key points.

DV made simple

Voiceover

A voiceover is an audio track of a person or persons speaking, heard above any background sound or music, which is played on top of a video segment.

Panning

A filming technique where the camera moves across a scene in a horizontal direction. You should pan in one direction only, i.e. do not pan back across the scene.

Working with native speakers

If you do not have the opportunity to film in the target language country, do you have a Foreign Language Assistant or native-speaker colleague or friend or parent who is willing to be filmed? Such video material not only brings a second, native-speaker voice into the classroom, it also provides lip synchronisation and natural gesture, and can be created to match exactly your Scheme of Work. Material might include:

- speeches to camera, about likes and dislikes or daily routine;
- show and tell presentations on hobbies or the place he or she comes from;
- close-up recital of the target language alphabet;
- animated recital of a poem;
- real interviews or imaginary interviews with the speaker playing, for example, a famous footballer or historical character.

Such material can be saved onto your network in a shared area for use by colleagues, but check on any capacity issues with your network manager. Some clips, such as the alphabet resource, could also be made available to pupils.

As you become more familiar with the functions of video editing, you can set up simple language learning activities, which require use of the software. For example, you can split a dialogue into separate clips and ask pupils to rearrange the clips into the correct order. Alternatively, you can ask pupils to write and record a voiceover for a video clip you provide of scenes around school or the local town.

Does digital video have a role in assessment for learning?

The flexibility and visual nature of digital video has great potential as an assessment for learning tool. Video provides a record of performance for review by teachers, peers and individuals, informing self-improvement and/or the next stage of a teaching sequence. A pupil watching him- or herself on video will appreciate, perhaps for the first time, how they sound to others when they speak the target language and the impact of body language and eye contact on the quality of communication. This record of achievement does not have to stand, however. A clip can be easily rerecorded and reviewed, with unwanted footage deleted at the editing stage. The *Evaluation report of the Becta digital video pilot project* states the following: 'that DV offers "feedback" to pupils was felt by teachers to have a significant impact on pupils' self-perception and self-esteem'. (Key finding 2.6, p7)

This cycle of review and improvement can be formalised into classroom activity. Where equipment is available, pupils can work in pairs, practising GCSE presentations or show and tell performances, taking it in turns to film and speak to camera. They can watch the recording together, reviewing pronunciation, fluency, accuracy, gesture and eye contact according to pre-agreed criteria, making decisions on what needs to be improved and redone.

Pupil efforts will be more focused if they are involved themselves in setting these quality criteria to which they work from the very start of an activity. A good starting point for establishing criteria is the National Curriculum levels for speaking in MFL, or a pupil-friendly version developed by the department. You could use a sorting activity, whereby pupils discuss statements and rearrange them into the correct order; or pupils could highlight key criteria for moving to the next level. You may want to add statements on quality of performance and presentation and, perhaps, originality, to allow scope for all pupils to achieve excellence.

Assessment for learning tasks may involve pupils working in pairs and you may not have enough access to video cameras to facilitate this. In such a case the teacher or Foreign Language Assistant could complete the filming with individual pupils while the class is working on another task. The clips can then be made available to pupils via the network; the network manager should be able to deliver clips to individual pupil areas if confidentiality is required. Again, peer review in pairs is likely to be most effective, and subsequent rehearsal and improvement of the presentations could result in selected performances to the class, depending on class size.

Alex Savage of Notre Dame High School has been researching the effective use of digital media as part of a Networked Learning Community project for the University of East Anglia. The peer assessment criteria developed with beginner learners are as follows, with pupils giving scores from 1 to 5:

If you can tell that they revised it	
Not looking at the book	
Sounds French (pronunciation)	
Flows well (fluent)	
Clear and confident	
Whole sentences	
Longer phrases	

The pupils made comments on their first experience of peer review when using digital video in language lessons, which included:

'I was really nervous doing it, but would be more confident next time.'

'I can see what I need to do to make it better.'

'I now understand how the teacher marks it.'

'It is easy to hear words that we say wrong.'

'It is good to learn from other people's mistakes.'

'I would only want to be videoed if I could do it well, so I would revise more before.'

To read more about Alex's preliminary work on the school website go to **www.ndhs.org.uk** and search on the key word 'video' to view his 'Effective uses of digital media' presentation.

Tile Hill Wood School, a participant in the CILT/BBC 21CC project, took a different approach, using a very open peer evaluation format for a Year 7 project:

I liked:
They could improve by:

Comments which emerged included:

> *'They used lots of Spanish.'*
>
> *'Watching both groups' videos gave us the chance to learn more things and to pronounce them.'*
>
> *'They could make it more interesting.'*
>
> *'They should talk a tiny bit louder.'*

Such reflections help to reveal to pupils how they can improve themselves. Their next task was the self-evaluation:

How well did I do?
I think I ...
I think I could ...
My targets are:

The video project and self-evaluation process led one pupil to comment: '... it was an interesting experience watching how I have progressed in this new language which I hadn't even thought about taking up'.

If you progress to an actual film-making project as discussed in Chapters 3 and 4, there is also potential for drawing up assessment levels which combine movie-making techniques and language skills. For some pupils, this could have a very positive impact on motivation and on their sense of achievement. The Digital Video in Education website offers a set of level descriptions for movie-making at the planning, filming and editing stages, which could act as a very good starting point (see the example on p16). This and many other useful guidance materials are available; go to **www.dvined.org.uk** > Downloads > Documents > Advice.

Movie Assessment Rubric

Level 2 Movie	Level 3 Movie	Level 4 Movie	Level 5 Movie
Planning			
Film does not fulfil the learning objectives	Film fulfils some of learning objectives	Film fulfils learning objectives	Learning objectives surpassed by film
Story line or content of film remains unclear	Evidence of storyline and content understandable	Clear storyline and one scene follows from another	Storyline that keeps viewer interested and amused
No real understanding of audience evident in film.	Some evidence of need to tailor film for audience	Clear evidence that film has been made for a specific audience	Film shows more than one example of catering for target audiences.
The film genre is unclear.	Film shows some leaning towards recognised genre	The film clearly fits into a specific genre	Film shows number of different aspects that associate it with specific genre

Source: © David Baugh, Digital Video in Education

The creation of video clips as a teaching resource for another class provides a particularly effective focus for such reflective classroom activity, as pupils will want to be satisfied with the finished product if it is to be used with their peers. Where pupils are working in groups, with defined roles such as actors, cameraman, director and lighting coordinator, the additional peer pressure element should encourage the review of linguistic performance, with footage being reshot until of adequate quality.

What hardware, software and other equipment do I need?

Before planning how to use digital video in the languages classroom, start off by finding out what facilities are going to be available to you in your school. Check with your ICT co-ordinator and/or network manager to find out what equipment already exists, either as a whole-school resource or housed within a department, such as ICT, Media Studies, Design Technology or Science. If your school is in an Excellence in Cities area, check whether you have access to a City Learning Centre (CLC), which can provide state-of-the art ICT learning facilities to local schools and the wider community.

Detailed technical guidance does not fall within the scope of this book, but to give a few pointers, the basic equipment requirements for digital video filming and editing are:
• digital video camera with 'DV out'
• **Firewire** input on your computer;
• video editing software;

Recommended extras are:
- external microphone;
- headphones;
- tripod.

DV made simple

Firewire
This technology enables the transfer of digital video footage from one device to another. It is also known as IEEE 1394 or i.Link. More modern computers have a Firewire **port** available, but otherwise you need to purchase and install a Firewire card.

Port
A socket on a computer to which cables for other devices are attached and through which data is sent and received.

Input and output devices
Video cameras can be purchased with different facilities for importing and exporting video data. For example, 'Analogue out' will allow you to plug your camera into a TV for playback. You need 'DV in' for importing edited video onto a camera for subsequent recording onto **VHS** (or you can connect to the VHS recorder directly if your computer has video output).

VHS (Video Home System)
This is an analogue, non-digital video format.

Importing and exporting
This is the opening and saving of a copy of a file you are working on, but in a different file format, so that it can be read by a software application or device different from that used to create the original file.

DV and mini DV format
DV is a very commonly used video format which uses tape cassettes. Mini-DV tapes (and cameras) are usually smaller than other DV tapes.

Although digital video cameras have become fairly widespread in recent years, both in homes and in schools, many digital stills cameras are also capable of recording a short amount of video footage of respectable quality. If you plan to purchase a digital video camera, you will need to make a number of decisions. Many cameras use **miniDV** format, but you will also come across Digital 8 format on Sony products. You will need to think about which **input** and **output device**s you require – do you need to play your video via a TV, for example? Digital video cameras should at least come with a Firewire cable to allow you to connect to a computer. Sound will be crucial for language learning activities, so you need to check that sockets are available for microphones and headphones. Some schools, particularly at primary, have invested in 'Digital Blue' Digital Movie Creator cameras. These are good value and robust cameras, capable of recording up to four minutes of footage, which come with their own easy-to-use editing software. While such low capacity in terms of time may limit the scope of video work possible, these cameras may be adequate for your purposes.

Media Education Wales provides an excellent overview of digital video camera and other equipment required and recommended for Media Studies, including pricing information. See **www.mediaedwales.org.uk/videokit.htm**. The Digital Media Community at Becta is a useful support network on technical matters (**http://schools.Becta.org.uk** > Get involved > Communities).

Once you have your hands on a camera, you need to learn how to use it. Fortunately, the simplest functions are all you need for point and shoot work, namely to:
- insert a tape into the camera, where applicable;
- use the **zoom** button to frame your shot;
- press the **record** button to start filming;
- press the **stop** button when you have finished the shot;
- use a tripod, if available, to avoid excessive wobbling;
- use headphones and an external microphone, if available, to ensure better sound quality (some teachers have found tie-clip microphones very useful).

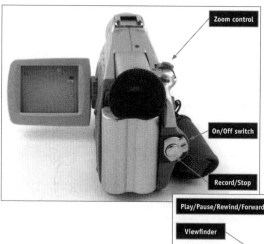

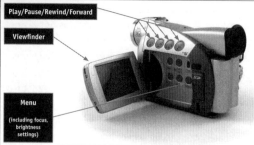

When you have finished filming, your network manager should be able to help you to identify an appropriate computer with Firewire input, onto which you can **capture** your video footage. He or she will recommend a computer with maximum **processor speed**, **RAM** and hard disk space, which can cope with capturing and editing video without problems. Many new computers come with a Firewire port, or you can buy the necessary card. If you purchase editing software, it often comes with a complimentary Firewire card.

DV made simple

Capturing
The process of downloading or transferring video footage from your camera or tape onto a computer; this process sometimes takes place in real time.

RAM (Random Access Memory)
The computer memory used by programs to perform tasks while the computer is running; when the computer is turned off, RAM loses its data.

Processor speed
The speed at which the 'brain' of the computer can work; the processor controls the execution of program instructions.

Video work requires an especially powerful computer, so there may be a dedicated machine for this purpose in your school. If you have a local City Learning Centre, you may find that there is a small cluster of dedicated machines, often Apple Macs offering iMovie software. Digital video technology is advancing all the time, but should you progress to running film-making projects with pupils, be aware that it may not be possible for 30 pupils to work simultaneously at individual machines.

There are a number of software options available when you come to edit your video footage, many of which are free. If you buy a Firewire card to enable your computer for video input, for example, it is likely to come packaged with editing software. PCs with Windows XP or later offer Movie Maker. Departments such as Design Technology or ICT may have purchased more sophisticated software, such as Pinnacle Studio or Adobe Premiere. If purchasing software, find out whether educational discounts are available and make sure that the software is compatible with your Firewire input.

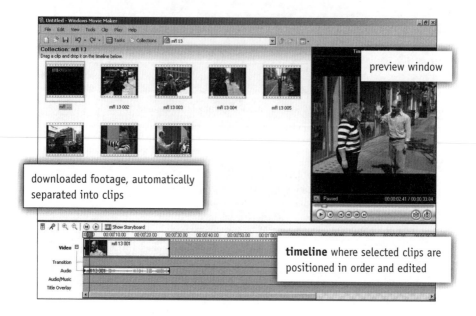

Source: Windows Movie Maker software interface

Finally, there are options available for converting **analogue** video footage to digital format, using an **ADC**. Once the footage is downloaded onto your computer, it can be manipulated and edited as with any digital video.

DV made simple

Analogue
A non-digital video format, such as VHS.

ADC (analogue-to-digital converter)
Either a converter card for your computer or an external adapter, both of which are reasonably cheap. It converts an analogue signal to digital so that video can be stored and processed by a computer.

Timeline
A window in editing software that displays a video project in a linear fashion horizontally across the screen. Clips are selected and positioned there in the order you require, appearing as different lengths according to their duration. Editing of clips takes place in the timeline; original clips remain available if needed.

What tips can I pick up on filming techniques and locations?

If you are doing simple point and shoot activities, your options for setting up an optimum filming environment will be limited. At a basic level, choose a brightly lit part of the classroom, but avoid shooting directly into the light. Try to minimise background noise; you may have to insist on a total silence policy while you are filming. A good strategy is to count down from 5, in the target language of course, but using only fingers for 3-2-1. Start filming when 3 is indicated and wait a few seconds at the end before pressing the **stop** button; this will help in producing video clips with smooth beginnings and endings. A clapperboard can be a fun addition to the process, but waiting three seconds before filming is still worth doing. Some cameras will allow you to replay what you have just recorded, but, as a general rule, do not try to rewind a tape to rerecord. Just keep going, you can edit out unwanted footage later.

Teachers at Brookvale High School provided 'job descriptions' to pupils working on their digital video project; you may find the guidelines for 'The camera operator' useful for quick reference.

The camera operator

- You must make sure the camera is switched on and then off to save power.
- You must hold the camera steady.
- You must ensure you are not filming into the light.
- You must **never** rewind the tape.
- You count the actors in 'five', 'four', (using fingers) 3, 2, 1.

If you are planning more ambitious video work, you may consider locations outside the classroom. Again, think about background noise as well as backdrop, as sound quality is paramount in MFL – so keep away from roads where possible. Even the sound of wind can affect the soundtrack. With a lot of video editing software it is possible to record the audio track again separately from the images once you have downloaded the footage onto your computer. Remember that you can insert still photos into a video sequence, so shots from the

21

target language country could enhance footage of pupils in front of neutral backdrops. The use of simple props can also really help to enhance the experience and the final product.

Health and safety is paramount, so keep away from any traffic routes in the school grounds and any sharp drops where pupils could be in danger of walking backwards over the edge. If pupils are working away from the teacher, a clear policy is needed on how they will be supervised. Should you plan to take pupils offsite, a new level of permissions will be required for filming (see Chapter 3 for details).

As your filming goes beyond the point and shoot level, keep in mind basic techniques for creating useful and effective footage.

- Aim for a finished product of around just one minute long, as a general rule. The combination of visual and audio means that video is a great communicator and short clips can be extremely effective. If you plan something much longer, you could get bogged down in excessive editing.
- Avoid excessive use of **panning** shots and pan in one direction only.
- Avoid using the **zoom** facility while you are filming; this is best used to **frame** your shot before you start.
- If filming in several locations, try not to mix different kinds of light, such as sunlight and artificial light. Avoid filming into the light also.
- Use of a tripod will help to minimise camera shake.
- Make sure that you monitor the sound being recorded through your headphones.
- If filming pupils, consider whether communication would be more natural if they did not look directly at the camera.
- Ask pupils to hold their position after they stop speaking for a couple of seconds, which will help at the editing stage.
- If you intend to edit together a number of clips, you do not need to film the clips in order, but do keep **continuity** in mind, especially of clothes and hair styles. If a pupil is wearing a sweater in an early clip, for example, make sure that it is still worn when another scene is filmed later in the day or week.

DV made simple

Zoom

Usually keeping your camera stationary, use the zoom lens on a camera to zoom in or out on the subject, to see more detail or to get a more overall view. Should not usually be used during filming; use it to frame your shot before you press record.

Framing

When you frame a shot, you not only decide what will and will not be included in the clip, you also decide how close your subject is to the camera and from what angle you will film. These choices affect what your film clip will communicate to its audience.

Panning

A filming technique where the camera moves across a scene in a horizontal direction. You should not change direction and pan back the way you have come.

Continuity

The process of ensuring that the visual aspects of a film are consistent from one take to the next. In the context of lesson work, the continuity person would be needed during filming to concentrate mostly on clothes, hairstyles, items held in hands and the background, although lighting and the **180 degree rule** are also considerations for more advanced users. There is also a continuity role during editing, ensuring that the edited sequence can be accepted by the audience as a natural sequence of action. The use of **cutaways** helps to achieve this.

Cutaway

A camera shot of something other than the principal action, perhaps of something being talked about or of someone listening, which is usually followed by a cutback to the first shot. Such shots are often used to disguise edits made to the original flow of action. The original soundtrack would usually play throughout the scene.

180 degree rule

A film editing guideline which stipulates that objects or people in a scene should always have the same left-right relationship to one another, whatever the position of the camera, to avoid disorientating the audience.

10 top tips for using DV on the Digital Video in Education website is an easy-to-understand introduction to effective filming. Go to **www.dvined.org.uk** > Downloads > Documents > Advice

How can I develop my understanding of the medium of film?

As you become more familiar with the camera and what you can do, you will no doubt start to expect to produce more sophisticated footage. This requires understanding of shot types and how film communicates meaning, which is a very interesting area offering many creative opportunities.

Once you have exhausted point and shoot activities, take some time out to watch a few minutes of a TV drama or other professional video sequence and note how they use camera shots to communicate to the audience. You will notice that the same scene is often viewed from different positions. Similarly, the camera will sometimes show a close-up shot of one actor in a dialogue; then it will show a medium distance shot of this actor with another. In a different sequence, an actor may be filmed from below or above. Most importantly, a scene will consist of a variety of camera shots, however short it is. This type of analysis activity should begin to reveal to you the language of film, giving insights into how emotions are communicated by the use of certain camera shots and how the attention of the audience is captured. Young people are increasingly equipped with this so-called 'visual literacy', which you can explore both through viewing and creating film with your pupils.

Perhaps the key lesson for those starting out with digital video work, however, is the flexible chronology of film-making. It is entirely possible to film the last scene first, as long as continuity issues are considered. In the context of school, this flexibility is very advantageous, as you can work around pupil absences or unexpected room changes. As your editing skills become more advanced, you can move from the point-and-shoot approach to more sophisticated filming. When recording a dialogue, for example, you should not film both people speaking in one long take from one camera position. A much more interesting and natural sequence will result if you film the conversation with the camera focused on one person; then film it again, focusing on the second person. Useful repetition for language learners! You should also make sure that you film extra footage of each person 'listening', clips known as **cutaways**. The video clips can then be reconstructed into the required order at the editing stage, providing a varied sequence of shots and giving you the option of using a cutaway, should the visuals of one clip be unusable for whatever reason. Should bits of the audio tracks be unusable, it is much easier to rerecord a few seconds of audio, than to set up a second filming session. Filming in this way requires an awareness of the **180 degree rule**.

The evaluation of the Becta project discovered that:

> *The most impressive pieces were informed by a sense of how to use the medium and the language of the moving image thoughtfully and deliberately, regardless of the curriculum area being supported.*

(Key finding 3.4, p8)

The report goes further to highlight that: 'The most potent use of DV is as a medium of expression and communication' (Key finding 1.4).

This last comment relates specifically to instances where the language of the moving image is fully embraced by teachers and pupils. Clearly, there is huge potential for bringing together the communication elements of both Modern Foreign Languages and Media Studies disciplines, which is explored further in Chapter 3. Digital Video in Education offers an illustrated information sheet called 'Learning about film language', which gives a very clear introduction to the language of film. Go to **www.dvined.org.uk** > Downloads > Documents > Advice.

Key points

- Start small!

- Get your ICT co-ordinator or network manager on board from the start – you will need him or her! Do a full test-run with the hardware and software, both to gain confidence in your skills and to ensure the school system can cope with what you plan to do.

- Set activities which have a clear focus and share the learning objectives, some of which will relate to social gains as well as language learning, with pupils.

- Remember that the greater your appreciation of the medium of film, the better the quality of your final product and the greater the benefit to pupils from the experience.

- If involving pupils in filming, allow them as much independence in and ownership of the process as possible.

Chapter 2
» Developing your material

- What do I need to consider when editing digital video clips?

- How can I incorporate digital video clips into my teaching resources?

- What role can more advanced editing features play in language learning?

- How can I exploit finished material as a teaching resource?

What do I need to consider when editing digital video clips?

This chapter focuses on the stages following your point and shoot activities, exploring ideas for how to make the most of the footage you have created in your teaching. The moving image is a powerful medium and can be a highly motivating and supportive classroom resource for target language work. You may want to integrate your simple filmed sequences into existing teaching resources, such as a PowerPoint presentation or interactive whiteboard slide, or they may form the basis of a new resource. Or you may simply want to play a video clip in isolation, or make individual clips available to different pupils. Whatever your immediate aspirations, knowledge of simple editing techniques will greatly improve the level of sophistication and flexibility of your footage. You may hit technical hitches as you proceed, but do not be too discouraged. Keep in close contact with your network manager, there are always several ways of solving problems.

Before you can begin editing, you need to transfer the footage onto your computer through the process called **capturing** (see p19). Complete all the filming you want to do for a particular activity or group of pupils first. Watch the footage through while still on the camera to get an overview of what sections you will want to include in your final edit. The editing software will keep all these related clips together as a **project**, from which you can create any number or length of video sequences, which you then save – each with their own file name – on your computer or network.

Attach your camera to the computer on which you are going to do your editing using the cable provided with the camera or Firewire card. If your computer is not powerful enough, you risk losing or distorting sections of your footage during the capturing process. Furthermore, your editing software may not work properly if your computer is inadequate to the task, so make sure you have consulted your network manager about which computer to use.

DV made simple

Digital video project

This is not a video file, it is a record of the clips you have selected and edits you have made. In Windows Movie Maker software, for example, projects have the file extension .MSWMM (Microsoft Windows Movie Maker). When you have finished editing, you create actual video by **exporting** (see p17) your work as a video file, which would have the file extension .WMV (Windows Media Video), for example.

The editing software on your computer will import the footage as one project, but will usually separate it out into all the different clips you filmed. Each clip will be displayed as a thumbnail, usually with a clip number; you can click on a clip to play it or drag it into the timeline (see p20). It is a good idea to give a name to each clip you select, particularly with dialogue, to make the editing process easier. This can actually be done while the footage is still on the camera with some camera models.

Whatever video clip(s) you place in the timeline can be edited and then saved or exported as an actual video file. The project file cannot usually be opened in any other software and is not a video file in itself. Clips added to the timeline are not deleted from the project, so if you change your mind about your edits later on, you can start again with the original clip, without having to repeat the capturing process.

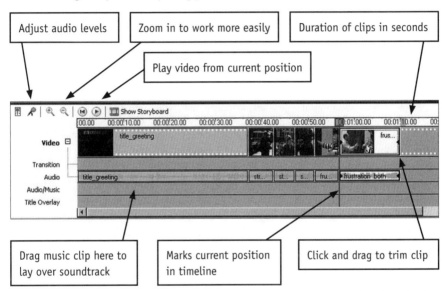

Source: Timeline in Windows Movie Maker software interface

So what edits will you do? At the simplest level, you can isolate a particular clip by adding it to the timeline and then saving it as an individual video file. In Movie Maker, you would simply go to File > Save Movie File. You can also top and tail this single clip to get rid of excess and spoiled footage, in a process known as **trimming**. This is usually done by dragging the start line across the clip thumbnail within the timeline. You will need to **zoom in** on a clip to make the timeline larger for more exact trimming. You can also **cut** footage from the middle of a clip, which in effect creates two clips.

An area which can become rather complex is deciding in which file format to save your video clips. The decision is usually a compromise between video quality and flexibility. Higher quality video means larger files, which may be impractical for your purposes, and you also need to consider within which contexts and applications you will want to play the video. See Appendix 1 for more information.

Once you can add a clip to a timeline, zoom in on it, trim it and save it as a video file, you can move onto more sophisticated work. A key issue for language teachers is the quality of the sound. Depending on the software you are using, you can usually both adjust sound levels within a clip by adjusting the Master Volume and clean up the sound by removing background noise. Another possibility is to edit the soundtrack separately in sound editing software, such as the free Audacity (**http://audacity.sourceforge.net**).

As you progress further and start to sequence a number of clips together, you can add **transitions** between clips, such as **fade to black** or **dissolve**. Transitions help to create a smooth and more professional-looking product, but be careful not to overdo them! Where you are working with a sequence of clips, try to keep sound levels consistent.

DV made simple

Cutting
Deleting a section of footage from any part of a video clip; the term 'cut' usually refers to the end of the clip.

Trimming
Editing or cutting a video clip to remove excess footage at the start and end.

Zoom in/out
Here, this refers to magnifying the view of the timeline in editing software, so that you can manipulate the software tools more easily to edit by the second of footage.

Transition
The movement from one clip to the next in a sequence of film. The end and start of two clips can be blended to smooth out the cut, using a dissolve, fade out, fade in, etc. effect.

Memory stick
Type of transportable data storage device, about the size of a stick of chewing gum, which plugs into a USB port on your computer. Available in a range of sizes, such as 32MB, 256MB, 2GB, this type of device has largely replaced the floppy disk, which could only hold 2MB of data. Similar devices are DiskGo or USB Flash Drive.

Do remember to save regularly and back up your work as often as possible, however. Your project file will remain small in size, but needs access to the original video footage. If there is limited space on your computer or hard drive, your project could access the video from elsewhere; some **memory sticks** are large enough to hold video, for example, or you can burn onto a writeable CD or DVD. Some people choose to purchase a separate hard drive. If you are working on a more ambitious project in which you are bringing together a large number of clips to create a professionally-produced film, note that the process can be very time consuming. You need both to manage your expectations of quality and to be organised, planning your edits on paper first if you can.

The Digital Video in Education (**www.dvined.org.uk**) website offers a range of very useful tutorials on using different video editing software packages.

How can I incorporate digital video clips into my teaching resources?

As you collect a bank of high-quality edited video clips of your holiday abroad, your FLA or your pupils, you will be in a position to select sequences with appropriate content and language level for particular lessons you plan to teach. Clearly, if you have used learners as 'actors' and intend to use footage as a learning resource for others, you also need to be satisfied with the quality of the pronunciation!

Playing from file

Unlike analogue video, digital video is very versatile and can be incorporated easily and effectively into a range of teaching resources. The simplest option is to play a video file from network or CD or memory stick, via a freely available **media player** such as Windows Media Player or QuickTime. Such a media player will offer you control buttons, such as Play, Pause, Stop, Forward and Rewind, as well as volume controls.

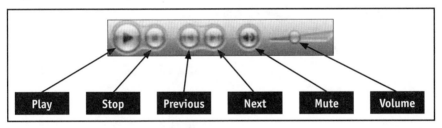

If you do not have an interactive whiteboard or spare board space, and/or you want to make notes alongside your video which you can save, there is a makeshift solution. Open your media player and Word (or another word-processing package) and size both windows so that both are visible on the screen at the same time. You can then type into the word-processing package while the video plays alongside it.

Playing from a presentation

An alternative is to play a video file from within **presentation software**, such as MS PowerPoint, allowing you to bring teaching resources together for a multimedia and more seamless delivery. Pupils can, for example, read target language text, view a still image, follow a link to a web page or click to hear a sound file or to watch a video file from within a single resource. The combination of text, audio and video/audio in this way can be a useful alternative if you have not yet progressed to video editing skills such as adding titles, inserting stills or adding audio tracks. The distinguishing feature of presentation software is that content and means of delivery are decided in advance; the answer to a question can be programmed to appear on the click of a mouse accompanied by the sound of applause, for example, which can be motivating for pupils. You can either embed a video file within PowerPoint using the **Pack and Go** function or link out to a file saved on your computer or network.

To give an example of using presentation software, take a simple observation and prediction activity:

- Display a **still frame** from the video clip on a PowerPoint slide, together with appropriate questions in the target language which can be imaginative, predictive and/ or factual and which require justification. The class shares speculative answers, which are noted on the ordinary whiteboard or paper flipchart

- What can you see?
- Where do you think they are?
- How do you know?
- What is the girl wearing?
- Who is she talking to?
- How old is the man?
- How is he feeling?
- What has he done?
- What will he do next?

Displaying a frame and questions using a PowerPoint slide

- Progress to the next slide, which displays the same questions and a sound icon linking to an audio file of the video soundtrack. Click on the sound icon and pupils listen to the soundtrack, subsequently revising their speculations on the board.
- Finally, you click for the pupils to watch the video, after which all answers can be confirmed, displayed on a final pre-prepared PowerPoint slide. This type of activity can lead into many types of writing and speaking activities, such as performing a role play of the video sequence or writing a dialogue on a similar theme.

You can obtain additional flexibility by using the **Windows Media Player Control**, which offers a control panel in the video window of your presentation, allowing you to pause or replay small sections and fast forward. Some people have met problems when playing back video within PowerPoint. This is often due to the video card on the computer, which needs to be able to support dual display of graphics. The Microsoft website offers useful and up-to-date guidance on this and other issues.

DV made simple

Media player

A piece of application software for playing back multimedia files, both audio and video, in a range of different formats. This software, such as Windows Media Player or QuickTime, is usually provided as part of your operating system. Alternative free programs can be downloaded from the web. The software usually includes control buttons, such as Play, Pause, Volume, etc.

Pack and Go

A facility within MS PowerPoint software that allows you to embed a video file within a presentation without the need to link out to a separate video file. This is useful if you need to use the presentation on different computers. See the File menu in PowerPoint.

Presentation software

An application, such as MS PowerPoint, used to create slide shows or multimedia presentations. Its unique feature is that you can easily pre-programme text and images to arrive in a certain order and style, including animation and sound effects. Most applications also offer a simple graphics system to create charts and graphs from inputted data.

Still frame

One of the many still images which compose a moving picture. If you do not have a 'camera' tool in your interactive whiteboard software you can create a still frame by pausing your video clip and pressing the Print Screen key on your keyboard. This copies an image of your entire screen to the clipboard. Paste the image into Word or PowerPoint and use the Crop tool on your Picture Toolbar to reduce the screen image to just the video still.

Windows Media Player Control

Media Player controls which toolbars can be made available within applications such as MS PowerPoint. Go to View > Toolbars > Control Toolbox within PowerPoint to bring up the Control Toolbox Toolbar. Click on the 'More Controls' icon and select 'Windows Media Player'. Drag your mouse to create a video window of the size you prefer. In the Control Toolbox Toolbar, click on 'Properties' and type in the location of your video file (e.g. C:\My documents\busqueda.mpg) in the URL box.

Playing from an interactive whiteboard slide

Teachers with an interactive whiteboard in their classroom will have access to proprietary software, such as SMART Notebook or ACTIVStudio2. Such software offers similar multimedia benefits as mentioned above for presentation software, but with greater flexibility and much easier manipulation of video and image, as well as additional facilities.

For example, video controls usually appear automatically, allowing you to pause and rewind whenever you like. You can also pause the video and very easily create a still image by taking a 'photo' of a given area of the screen. Depending on which software you are working with, you can make both handwritten or typed notes and annotations alongside or over the video as it plays. These notes can be saved for future consultation and editing or printing out.

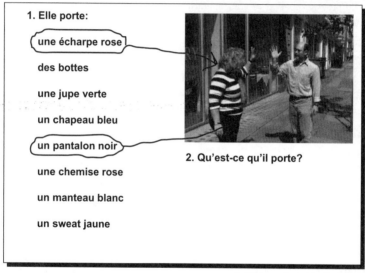

A still image from video footage, with notes

There is often a spotlight function for use with active or paused video, where a black layer covers your screen except for a 'hole' which reveals the action underneath. This is very useful for brainstorming and using speculative language (see example of teacher questioning opposite). Similarly, there is a 'blind' you can use to reveal the action from any direction, in the same way that you would use a piece of paper to reveal an OHT. It is worth exploring the software which comes with your interactive whiteboard to find out what is possible.

The spotlight function reveals part of the action.

Playing video from a web page

Making video available via a web page has the advantage of being accessible anywhere; by pupils for homework, by a partner school or by colleagues in school and beyond. Video files can be saved in different resolutions, giving access options to Internet users on different bandwidths. See the Royal Grammar School example on p8. Clearly, pupil protection is a critical issue and great care should be taken to avoid giving any information about a pupil which might identify him or her. You can combine text, images and/or audio files alongside a video clip on the same web page; it is usually possible to include a video control panel also. Web pages can be created in software such as Microsoft Front Page or Dreamweaver, which are very likely to be available in school. As always, consult your network manager or school webmaster.

What role can more advanced editing features play in language learning?

Basic editing to make the most of point and shoot footage need only consist of topping and tailing clips and saving in an appropriate format. As your skills become more advanced, however, you can take further advantage of the medium to maximise language learning opportunities. Most notably, you can exploit the use of text and audio alongside the moving image, to create teaching resources or set up learning activities which appeal to a wider range of learning styles.

Brookvale High School summarised the editor role for their project work as follows:

The editor

- 🎥 You decide which shots to use.
- 🎥 You trim the raw film to leave just the best bits.
- 🎥 You add titles and credits.
- 🎥 You clean up the sound.
- 🎥 You add special effects.

Working with text

Titles can be used over the moving image, over a still image or against black, in any position on the screen. Possible applications include:

- film title;
- **inter-titles** as introduction to set the scene;
- **sub-titling** of the video dialogue;
- device for setting a new scene within a storyline;
- text to accompany a music-only soundtrack;
- translation of key words;
- text-based commentary or translation of dialogue to create a bilingual resource;
- credits listing names against film-making roles in the target language.

The inclusion of text within a video resource can support language learners with a more visual learning style and help to build pupils' confidence in listening, as well as reinforcing the sound–spelling link. You could also store a copy of the clip without sub-titling, enabling you to remove support gradually. Where pupils are creating material themselves, sub-titling provides a new context and additional practice for writing. As with the dialogue, knowing that others are to watch their work, there is likely to be an extra effort to ensure the accuracy and quality of the text.

> ## DV made simple
>
> ### Titles
> Text which appears on screen over still images, empty screen or moving video. Credits or text to set the scene are sometimes known as inter-titles. Sub-titles appear along the bottom of the screen over moving video, as a summary, translation or visual display of the dialogue.
>
> ### Noise removal
> You can remove unwanted background noise from the soundtrack to a video clip; often this needs to be done in audio editing software, such as the freeware Audacity. Removal of a persistent noise is done by identifying a tiny section of the audio track where just the offending sound can be heard, which the software then strips from the entire soundtrack.
>
> ### Voiceover
> A voiceover is an audio track of a person or persons speaking, heard above any background sound or music, which is played on top of a video segment. It can give the audience information difficult to dramatise, such as the background to the story, the thoughts of a character or the passage of a long period of time. Usually no attempts are made to match onscreen lip movement, but the length of a voiceover must not be longer than the video sequence.

Working with audio

Much editing software offers the facility for multi-track audio, which means that a voice track can be played simultaneously over a recording of natural background sound and over a music soundtrack, for example. The more you become familiar with the rules of film-making and understand how film communicates meaning, the better placed you will be to decide upon dialogue, voiceover, or a mixture of the two. If you concentrate on dialogue, you may find that the original voice track is too poor quality to be heard clearly, but the facility for cleaning it up or **noise removal** is often possible. If this does not work well enough, a second option is to rerecord the dialogue as an audio file. If a lack of lip synchronisation becomes a problem at a particular point, remember that the video can show the listener's reaction, or the back view of the person speaking, as long as the mood of the scene is not adversely affected by this. As a last resort, the dialogue could cut to a narrator's voiceover, filling in the information missed.

Another approach is to film footage to which you will add a **voiceover**. This ideally requires planning, writing and rehearsal of the voiceover text in advance of filming to allow you to plan appropriate content and length of the footage you film. Clearly, this could be an excellent target language activity for pupils. An alternative activity is to provide footage you have filmed yourself and ask pupils to write and perform a voiceover to complement it.

Arguably, a voiceover could require a much greater range of language and opportunities for use of voice tone and expression to communicate the factual and emotional context of a scene than straightforward dialogue.

It is also possible to add a music soundtrack, which will help to communicate mood or context. You can fade a track in and out according to what is happening in your video. Do consider copyright, however, particularly if you intend to show your video outside the classroom. The government's Intellectual Property Office website (**www.ipo.gov.uk**) gives some guidance, but copyright is not a straightforward and definitive area; the best advice seems to be to play safe and contact copyright holders for permission before using any music clip. You could also explore sources of free music clips, such as **www.flashkit.com** and the Downloads area of the Digital Video in Education website. If your video project is more ambitious and deals with more complex emotions and situations, you could consider approaching the music department to work together to create a soundtrack.

Working with graphics and special effects

If you have lots of time to spend on your video project and/or you need to communicate a particular message, your editing software should offer you a range of useful options. A simple but effective technique is the use of stills, which can originate from the video footage, from digital photos or scanned images. Royal Grammar School, for example, used a photo of a restaurant taken on a school trip to Germany and inserted it before a scene in German in the school canteen back in the UK, creating the impression that the pupils were in Germany. Brookvale High School used an effect where mesmerising stars and bubbles filled the screen, complete with appropriate sound effect, in their story about a fortune-teller; this gave the impression of magic as she disappeared to leave nothing but her glass ball (also an editing trick, of course!). You can usually 'age' the look of video footage, right down to full sepia effect, useful if you are working on a target language history project. If your dialogue is more imaginative and a pupil is having a conversation with an alien creature, for example, an image of the creature can be added to a video sequence. Do ensure, however, that any titles or graphics you use will not disappear off the edge of the screen.

Text, audio and graphics can be combined in diverse ways with the moving image to create a final product with variety and appeal for any audience. With such creative, technical and communication skills employed in editing, it obviously has much to offer pupils. As reported in the Becta DV pilot, one teacher was quoted as saying: 'Editing is for them [the pupils] a fantastic critical judgement about what they've done; it's an evaluation'. In MFL terms, it is also listening practice and repetition, and where clips are rerecorded or voiceovers created, it becomes further speaking and pronunciation practice. Examples of projects where pupils create and edit their own digital video are explored in detail in Chapters 3 and 4.

> **DV made simple**
>
> **Safe area**
>
> The portion of the picture, to which important visuals, action, or titles should be confined, so that nothing vital is lost if played on a TV with significant overscan. (TVs overscan so that the screen is filled and there are no black borders.) Editing software tends to show the whole picture in the viewing window and sometimes indicates the safe area for you. The term is also used to describe the area beyond that seen through the camera viewfinder, where a microphone can be safely held.

How can I exploit finished material as a teaching resource?

Many language teachers are already well-practised in exploiting the moving image in the classroom and many of these techniques can be applied to the use of digital video clips you have created as a teaching resource, depending on the nature of the clip. To summarise a few of these techniques:

- Prepare keyword cards for a sequence of video and hand out to pupils. When a pupil hears the word written on his/her card, he or she holds the card up in the air. An alternative is to give each pupil several cards, so that he or she has to select the correct one each time.
- Let pupils watch a video clip without sound and guess what is going on, developing language and ideas for the scene; this can then lead into a written activity or an oral performance. Of course, you can simply replay the scene with sound as a listening activity and compare with class notes.
- Alternatively, blank the screen so that only the soundtrack can be heard. Pupils speculate as to what is going on in the clip and where, and/or summarise what was said. As a drama and listening activity, pupils could act out their imagined scene to the soundtrack, or ad-lib a dialogue to the visual sequence.
- Where a clip has a clear context or storyline, ask pupils to guess what came before the chosen scene or what will happen after, as an opportunity to practise different tenses and think imaginatively in the target language. Pupils can also identify one character and write what they would do in the future if they were that person, using the conditional tense.
- Use techniques from listening comprehension, such as gap-fill, gist and detail note-taking and text reordering, which can work more effectively with moving images as the pupils have a clear visual clue as to who is speaking and the context they are in. Gap-fill activities could be presented as an incomplete storyboard, rather than simple text.
- Where you have more sophisticated video clips at your disposal, you can set up activities with lists of statements, such as reordering and true-false.

The British Film Institute publishes *Moving images in the classroom*, a useful handbook which is free to schools and includes ideas for exploiting digital video clips you have created as a language teaching resource. It is available to download from **www.bfi.org.uk/education/ teaching/miic/**.

Key points

- Be prepared to call on technical support throughout the different stages of digital video work; the diversity of file types and demands on computer capacity and memory can cause problems which are surmountable but can bring you to a full-stop at any point. Don't struggle alone!

- Consider carefully how and to what learning ends you will exploit your finished clips with pupils before you decide to invest time editing, and select the appropriate technical medium for dissemination.

- Even simple editing can greatly enhance the quality of digital video footage and therefore the possibilities for classroom application. More advanced editing can help to produce some of the richest learning resources available to us as teachers. Develop your skills over time and don't give up!

- Remember that editing is the most time-consuming element of digital video work. Set yourself realistic goals and be ready to manage pupils' expectations when they are creating their own video.

- Be imaginative! A single video clip can be used in a plethora of ways to support language learning across all four skills for pupils of different ages and abilities.

Chapter 3
» Planning film-making projects

- What is the rationale for setting up a film-making project with pupils?

- What is the relationship between the film-making process and language learning?

- What nature should a project take?

- What logistical and health and safety issues should be considered?

- What are some good ideas for a film project focus?

- How can I prepare my pupils for this new way of working?

What is the rationale for setting up a film-making project with pupils?

There is widespread evidence from the pilot that using DV dramatically increases the motivation for learning and engagement of a wide range of learners, but particularly those excluded from the traditional curriculum. Using DV as part of learning tasks improves behaviour and on-task concentration. Pupils are engaged to stay beyond lessons – into breaks, lunchtimes, and after school.

(Becta 2002)

With confidence in your own skills to film and edit digitally the next step could be to plan and implement a film-making project with pupils, in which they work independently. Handing the reins to pupils can seem risky but has enormous benefit for language work and for developing your pupils' creativity with the language, as well as their ability to work in groups, to make decisions and to problem-solve.

The study of modern foreign languages also has an important contribution to make to cross-curricular skills and competences. These skills include for example social, through communication and co-operation; personal, by developing creativity and imagination; study, through observation, research and planning using a variety of media; and vocational, through communicative competence, independence, problem-solving and decision-making.

(DfES 1990)

We have already mentioned the motivation inherent in using video material; both in watching and creating it, and the increasing **visual literacy** that young people are developing. We will also examine in this chapter the benefits to language learning from pupil-centred film-making. However there are further generic skills which pupils develop from this way of working, skills which have cross-curricular links and which can raise the status of MFL for pupils. Where the study of a foreign language is optional, it makes sense for teachers to look for ways which will add variety and interest to the language curriculum. We will see how these are skills which contribute to the development of the whole child.

DV made simple
Visual literacy
The ability to look at visual information with perception. A visually literate person understands how visual elements contribute to the meaning of the whole.

Here are some generic skills that pupils are developing during a digital video project:

- Pupils are being encouraged to deconstruct the process of making a film, to analyse shots and narrative and to imagine how they want their final product to look. They are making conscious use of their visual literacy and extending their knowledge of visual media.
- Pupils are working in groups. You may want to outline the roles and responsibilities within the groups, however essentially the pupils have to collaborate and communicate their ideas effectively.
- In group work pupils have to reach a consensus and take important decisions. They will motivate and inspire each other, but they may also criticise each other and become discouraged. This is a crucial area of learning to work in a group.
- The pupils will be working as independently as possible from the teacher. This can be a problematic area in MFL as there is often an over-reliance on the teacher's support. Pupils need to be encouraged to consult dictionaries, textbooks and on-line resources in order to work more autonomously. At the end of this chapter we will look in more depth at how teachers can support pupils in working in groups.
- Working independently and in groups means that pupils are using and developing their problem-solving skills, for example they will need to find ways to express their ideas in the target language and to solve technical issues during filming as well as disagreements that may arise in their groups.
- Pupils are encouraged to use their imagination and to be creative, not only by using their language creatively but also in the type of film they create.
- Pupils gain confidence in their ability to use the language they have learned in different contexts and to learn new skills, such as acting and presenting or their ICT knowledge.
- Pupils are acquiring new ICT skills, which can be used in other curriculum areas or in their home-life. These are practical skills that can be used and extended immediately. This can raise the status of MFL with some pupils, as they are acquiring other useful and immediately applicable skills. This is especially true for pupils who may struggle with the foreign language but are able to participate and be successful during a film-making project.
- The new ICT skills provide solid support for the ICT National Curriculum and can be a link into other ICT areas, for example making digital audio recordings, which involve similar skills.

The skills listed here have clear links with other national strategies in both the Primary and Secondary phases. In the Primary phase the principles of good teaching and learning set out in the document *Excellence and enjoyment: A strategy for primary schools* can be developed through work with digital video:

* ★ **Make learning vivid and real**: *develop understanding through enquiry, creativity, e-learning and group problem-solving.*
* ★ **Make learning an enjoyable and challenging experience**: *stimulate learning through matching teaching techniques and strategies to a range of learning styles.*
* ★ **Enrich the learning experience**: *build learning skills across the curriculum.*
* ★ **Promote assessment for learning**: *make children partners in their learning.*

(DfES, 2003)

In terms of the Secondary National Strategy we can see how pupil-centred film-making supports the development of thinking skills, which are in part of the 'Leading in learning: developing thinking skills at Key Stage 3' strand. If pupils are guided through the stages of making a digital video film and understand ways of working effectively in groups and developing language then this is part of their understanding of how they learn. In addition we have already looked at the potential for assessment for learning in using digital video. With pupil-made films it is particularly beneficial to make peer assessment one of the possible outcomes of a digital video project.

From the Becta pilot teachers described some of the impact the projects had for pupils: 'Pupils demonstrated increasing forward thinking/planning but also the will to change plans as circumstances and context changed'. Also, 'All of the students have had their self-esteem raised and are showing more signs of confidence in other areas of their education'.

What is the relationship between the film-making process and language learning?

[...] language is acquired most effectively when the learner, having rehearsed i.e., having learned his lines, an essential stage, otherwise he would have nothing to say, is able to concentrate on the performance, that is on the message, which must matter enough to him to divert this attention from the medium.

(Eric Hawkins 1987)

The desire to carry out a digital video project stems from understanding the benefits it will bring primarily to the pupils' language learning. We have already touched on the generic skills that will be reinforced in the process of making a film, such as working in a group and problem solving, and we will look at those areas in more detail later on in this chapter. For now, we should look at the language work which goes on during the process of planning and making a film. The crucial point is that pupils should be able to use the language they know in a context which has meaning for them. In this way the language may seem more 'real' to them and using it constitutes an actual 'performance' as opposed to endless language practice for the perhaps distant day when they have an opportunity to communicate with a native speaker.

- In the **planning** stage pupils are using known language creatively; they are reading and writing scripts, using dictionaries and textbooks to help them express their ideas. They may want to extend what they can say and to put language they have learned from a range of topics into different contexts.
- In the **rehearsal** stage pupils are committing language to memory and are motivated to do so, firstly because they have been part of composing the script and secondly because they want to achieve a good end result. Pupils undertake this intense language practice almost unaware of it as learning.
- During **filming** pupils are practising and repeating the language; by speaking, listening and correcting each other. They want to be more accurate and to sound more fluent. They also want to get the acting right or to get the right shot. In their rehearsals and repetition the language they have put together is refined and memorised.
- In the **editing** stage pupils are listening again to what they have recorded and may well be adding written language in terms of titles and **subtitles**. They may also record an audio voice over. They need to select the best and clearest versions of what they have recorded and so are making decisions about what constitutes clear and accurate oral production of the language.
- In **sharing** their results pupils are learning from each other's work as well as reinforcing and extending their language knowledge. They can also assess each other in terms of creativity, accuracy, clarity, production values, acting, etc.

DV made simple

Subtitles

The voice of an unseen narrator, or of an onscreen character not seen speaking. The translation of the dialogue if the film is in a foreign language.

What nature should a project take?

Before you start to plan a larger scale digital video project and before you even decide which class you are going to work with, you need to establish the level of support you can rely on from a range of colleagues and the availability of and access to appropriate hardware and software. Getting support from your school's senior management is crucial, not only in terms of procuring any necessary finance, but ensuring a sympathetic view when you need cover for lessons or training, or permission to take pupils out of lessons, and when you need to contact parents to get permission for pupils to be filmed. It will also help to disseminate the outcomes of the project at a whole school level if members of the senior management are kept involved in some way.

The scope of a digital video project can vary from being a modest undertaking to something much more substantial; it is possible to make a film with any year group and on any topic or language area. So once you are familiar with the technical set-up and potential limitations, the decisions about starting a film-making project begin with how to select the pupils to work with, what they will film and when they will do the filming and editing. A digital video project can become a standard part of a scheme of work and be completed in class time, but could also be part of the MFL department's extra-curricular activities.

The extra-curricular model of working has the advantage that pupils are generally self-selected and motivated. There is also less time pressure to complete the project. The pupils could be from your Gifted and Talented cohort or they may be pupils who can go on to become mentors or advisers to future projects with a larger number of participants. It would also be possible to have a mixed age group and to produce more special one-off digital video films. Several schools that took part in the CILT/BBC 21CC project took the pupils off timetable for a day or afternoon, in order to gain a more focussed approach. A disadvantage of these projects is that they have less connection to the curriculum, so they may suffer from poor attendance and a lack of continuity from one week to the next. Film-making projects completed outside the classroom can take on many different forms and serve a variety of purposes and audiences:

- as a way of linking with partner schools abroad. For example, one of the schools which took part in the CILT/BBC 21CC classroom project organised a trip to Germany in order to create a film with their partner school;
- as provision for Gifted and Talented students, at lunchtime or at the weekend;
- as a weekend activity for a film club;
- as provision for pupils with special educational needs;
- as an activity for a lunchtime club focussed on film-making or as a focus for an MFL club;
- as an end of year 'Activities Week' project;
- as part of the celebrations for the European Day of Languages;
- as a way of linking with a partner school in the UK;
- as a way of linking with another department area (see the King's Norton example later in this chapter);
- as a project to support cross-curricular themes, such as Citizenship.

Including a digital video project as part of a scheme of work is an effective way of embedding and disseminating film-making skills not only among pupils but also among the rest of the MFL department. It also ensures that the language used will be a reinforcement and extension of language from the curriculum for all pupils. At Shirelands Language College all Year 8 pupils are being given the opportunity to make a film in their MFL and Community languages lessons, regardless of the language they are learning and their level, as the film-making projects have been included in the Year 8 schemes of work.

However, there may well be constraints in terms of the time it takes to plan, film and edit a short film and in terms of access to technology for a whole class, or indeed year group. In the classroom, too, pupils need support to work in groups efficiently, and teachers may need an extra pair of hands to keep the groups on task and to supervise the language work as well as the more technical aspects of the process. An extra member of staff is also invaluable for ensuring that all group members are working equally and that they are using the target language as much as possible.

If you are filming outside the classroom, it will be essential to have an extra member of staff for reasons of health and safety. Possible extra members of staff could be:
• a foreign language assistant;
• a teaching assistant or higher-level teaching assistant;
• a Post Graduate Certificate of Education (PGCE) trainee or other trainee;
• an Advanced Skills Teacher (AST);
• a member of the ICT department;
• a member of the City Learning Centre (CLC) team.

Nevertheless the 'in-class' model of working can be successful, particularly when pupils are aware of the stages of the film-making process and are given strategies for working in groups and independently of the teacher. It may also help to have a stock of straightforward 'self-access' language worksheets for those pupils or groups who have finished or need to wait to go on to the next stage.

Whichever model of working you choose, setting a deadline for the completion of the film, especially if it is a celebration of some sort, will give a clear incentive for pupils to keep working and to deliver a final product. Bear in mind too that there are awards available from educational institutions, as well as awards from some of the larger cinema chains.

So once the decision has been made about why you are making a video, which pupils will be taking part in the project and when their work will take place, the next decision is what kind of film they will make. It may be that the kind of language you wish to practise with the class will dictate the genre. For example in the CILT/BBC 21CC project teachers at Brookvale School decided that they wanted to practise the language for role plays in the restaurant which dictated the kind of film the pupils were asked to produce.

Broadly speaking, the genre of film could be factual reporting or a work of fiction. For factual reporting some ideas relevant to MFL teaching are:
• weather forecast;
• news report;
• presentation of local area or school for an exchange group;

- documentary open/closing sequence;
- explanation of *faux amis* e.g *embarazada* = 'pregnant' not 'embarassed' in Spanish;
- recipe demonstration;
- interviews with real people;
- seeing the world 'through the eyes of another'
- teaching of a language point to a younger class.

For works of fiction, ideas specific to MFL teaching could be based on a TV or film format, or be more imaginative. Ideas for TV or film format include:
- TV advertisement;
- film trailer;
- film opening sequence;
- pretend interviews with real celebrities;
- talk show;
- reality show;
- soap opera;
- presentation of nominations at an Awards ceremony (i.e. short film clips, which come together to make one final product);
- TV programme formula (e.g. *Blind Date, Weakest Link, X Factor, Jerry Springer, Ready Steady Cook*).

Ideas that require more imagination include:
- dramatised role play;
- historical re-enactment;
- recreation of a scene in literature;
- voicing an animation sequence using pictures or objects;
- dramatisation of a poem;
- film of pupils' own creative work;
- pupils audition for the same part in a film;
- dream.

What logistical and health and safety issues should I consider?

Technical and logistical considerations are key to how you plan the project and what type of project you set up. Check with your ICT co-ordinator and/or network manager to find out what equipment and software the school has access to already. This dialogue should also reveal the skills you can expect from your various classes of pupils with regard to working a camera and editing digital video. Aside from the desirability of setting up group projects, it is unlikely to be possible to have pupils editing video at 30 terminals in the computer suite, because of the pressure such high-asset work would put on the server.

Once you have established the hardware and software you will be using, you need to consider the level of training you will need to facilitate the project with your pupils. Remember that you do not have to be the technical expert if you have managed to establish a successful collaboration with other colleagues.

The flexibility offered by new technologies brings with it potential concerns for pupil security and the legal protection of teachers. First and foremost, it is crucial to establish if you need to obtain parental permission for the filming you will be carrying out, bearing in mind how you will use the footage in the short and long term and how it will be stored. If you want to publish films on the school website or prepare video footage for your exchange partner school, then clearly there are issues which you need to pursue further; it may be that permission is requested from parents from the start for using material in a specific way. Some schools include general permission for filming and using pupils' images in their home school agreements.

We have some guidelines for a permission letter to parents in Appendix 2. With a class of 30 pupils it will take time to collect all the permission letters, so the process needs to begin several weeks before the planned filming, with the full knowledge and co-operation of the senior management. Up-to-date guidance on these issues can be found at the Becta website under 'Safety tips for digital video projects'.

You will also need to check carefully the school policy on taking pupils out of school if you wish to film off-site, and you may need to carry out a detailed risk assessment. You will need to establish how much extra supervision is required and to obtain parental permission for pupils to be working off-site.

The process of filming is exciting but also hazardous, as pupils are focussing on their acting or on their equipment and lose sight of what is around them. For a comprehensive list of do's and don'ts when filming, look at the Becta website under 'Safety tips for digital video projects' or in Appendix 3.

What are some good ideas for a film project focus?

The following are ideas for films from schools that took part in the CILT/BBC 21CC digital video project.

Brookvale High School

A lunchtime Digital Video Club was offered to Year 8 top sets in French and German. Using a single digital video camera and computer with Pinnacle Studio software, they worked to develop a French and a German teaching resource for their peers. They developed scripts on the theme of fortune-telling, using the future tense of the verb, to be, as the grammar focus of the resource.

Coombe Girls' School

Working with Year 8 French beginners in lesson time, this project involved the creation of a news programme for presentation at an end-of-year Performance Day. The class worked in groups and assigned roles to work on separate news items, which revised topics from the scheme of work. The pupils then edited their section using iMovie software on iMac laptops over two lessons, before bringing the final news programme together in the last lesson. They also created worksheets for their audience to complete during the performance.

Elizabeth Garrett Anderson School

Three Year 8 and three Year 9 girls were chosen from a large number of volunteers to take part in a Film Club pilot in lunchtime and after school. Given free choice on focus, they decided to write and film a role play in a real shop. A second project focused on poetry, combining illustrations, voiceover of the poem and hand-level footage of the writer penning the poem.

Ian Ramsey CE School

Working with equipment loaned by a local CLC, a German class filmed footage over the period of a week, recording key moments during an exchange visit by a German group to their school. The footage included interviews in both languages about what the children had purchased and their attempts at cooking. Bilingual subtitles were then added to the film, which will be used as a souvenir of the trip and for promoting the school locally.

Kings Norton Girls' School

A collaboration between the MFL and PE departments saw eight pupils taken out of lessons for two hours a week over half a term. Having brainstormed ideas around the health and fitness topic, the team built up the storyboard for their French film with the help of the FLA and other teachers. The resulting footage included shots from around the school of PE activities, with pupil voiceovers and brief interviews with staff members from all subject areas in the target language.

Prince Henry's Grammar School

Working with a Year 8 top set, the project aimed to create a teaching resource for other KS3 classes on the topic of daily routine. Having identified ten key actions, pupils developed storyboards in preparation for filming. They also wrote scripts for the voiceovers, which were added at a later date.

Purbrook Park School

This project focused on a large mixed ability Year 8 class and was aimed at improving motivation and classroom dynamics through the introduction of group working. Focusing on the topic of ordering food and drink in a café or restaurant, pupils worked collaboratively, with individuals having clear roles from the start. It was intended that completed footage be used as a teaching resource with other classes and that this type of working be extended throughout the department, including a project in Activities Week.

Queen Mary's High School

Two projects were developed, the first for a volunteer group of six Year 8 gifted and talented girls, all studying different languages. With the aim of introducing the school to new Year 7 pupils and various exchange schools, a flexible film with the potential for multilingual voiceover was envisaged. The girls worked mainly in their own time on scripts and storyboards for different sub-topics, with occasional meetings as a group and some off-timetable time for filming. A Year 9 Japanese class took part in the second project, using the last ten minutes of lessons supplemented by free time in school. Working in groups within the topic of education, they devised creative scripts and storyboards, such as 'A day in the life of a lost textbook' and a 'Blair Witch'-style sequence.

Royal Grammar School

A Year 9 German class of twelve boys developed a scenario dialogue in which one boy lost his glasses and went around the school looking for them. The joint writing exercise in class was supplemented by lunchtime planning for a half-day off timetable for filming around the school. Scenes were filmed in the school playground, swimming pool, library and canteen, and several members of staff were 'interviewed' in German as the boy searched for his glasses (which were on his head all the time!).

South Wolds School

A Year 7 fast-track French class and a Year 8 German class selected key figures from French and German life, and history, through a whole-class brainstorm, followed by Internet-based research. Characters ranged from Astérix, Patrick Vieira, Brigitte Bardot and Napoleon for French, to Carl Benz, Albert Einstein and Adolf Hitler for German. Pupils worked in small groups to devise questions and answers, and to practise an interview to be performed in front of the class, complete with props and costumes. Pupils agreed on evaluation criteria for choosing the best efforts. These were then performed again in front of the video camera in a subsequent lesson and volunteers completed editing in lunchtimes.

St Julie's Catholic High School

A Year 10 Spanish Set 2 used lessons and lunchtimes to develop a film introducing their school, working in groups to research and develop scripts focusing on different aspects of school life. Armed with permission slips, pupils visited classrooms and buildings around the school to create generic footage. They then worked on editing the clips into a coherent film complete with voiceover in Spanish.

Wirral Grammar School for Girls

This project built on an existing link with a local special school, in which Year 7 and 8 boys coming into the school to learn Spanish were brought together with able Year 10 girls who would act as peer mentors. Working in lunchtimes, they planned scripts together in English for their version of *Ghostbusters*, which were voted on to select the overall favourite. The girls then worked to translate different sections of the script into Spanish. The teacher suggested corrections and recorded a model reading to support the girls in coaching the boys. The Art and Technology departments helped to develop costumes, logos and 'equipment' for the filming and four girls with good technical skills completed the editing. Following the project, a Year 8 French class filmed their version of *Blind Date* and visited the local CLC for editing. A German group filmed different stages of the school building programme, which will be sent to partner schools with a voiceover in German.

The Holt School

A class of Year 9 pupils in German were given a free hand to use recently learned language for their short films. Several of the groups copied known TV formats, such as *X Factor* and *What Not to Wear*. Another group filmed the story of *Der Dieb* (the Thief) and followed the thief around school, stealing key items from teachers of different subjects. The teachers were played by pupils, some imitating teachers in the school, and they confronted the thief at the end of the film. The language focussed on asking where items were, using different prepositions and cases in German.The pupils edited their films using Windows Movie Maker and used CD-ROMs to store their films, replacing the new films on the CD each time they were edited. All the films were entered for a local school film competition and *Der Dieb* went on to win a prize.

Another group of Year 10 French pupils focussed on making short films around the topic my leisure. One group made simple paper models of snails and filmed their 'race', complete with commentary in French.

How can I prepare my pupils for this new way of working?

There are three key areas of preparation for pupils to ensure that the digital video project runs smoothly and that pupils get most benefit from it. These are: understanding how films are made; what language they should focus on and where to find support for their writing; and how to work effectively in a group.

Firstly, pupils will need to develop their film literacy. Most pupils are not likely to have had the opportunity to break down the process of film-making and will be unaware of how different shots, camera angles and effects are used when producing a film.

An effective exercise at the beginning of a film project can be to analyse a short piece of film to see how it was produced (see Film analysis sheet, p54). Pupils can be asked to look out for:
- the key idea of the sequence and the target audience;
- the number of shots required to complete the sequence;
- the use of different camera angles and what effect they had;
- the use of panning, zooming in and out and tracking shots, as well as close-ups and long or wide shots;
- the music or other voices/sounds on the soundtrack;
- the lighting, either indoor or outdoor;
- other additions, e.g. transitions between shots and subtitles.

DV Made Simple

Tracking
A movie shot made by a camera moving steadily on a track or dolly (a camera mounted on wheels) and following the action.

Close-up
A photograph or a film shot in which the subject is tightly framed and shown at a relatively large scale.

Long shot
Overall view from a distance of the whole scene, often used as an establishing shot to set the scene.

Wide shot
A shot of the whole scene, using a wide-angle lens.

Pupils could then be asked to complete a shot list, script and/or storyboard for the sequence used. All of these terms will be looked at in more detail on pp69–76 in Chapter 4. At this stage it may also be helpful to look at the flexible chronology of filming, i.e. that scenes can

Film analysis sheet

The opening sequence	✓ ✗	Why are they used?
The camera shots: • wide/long • close up • zoom in • zoom out • pan • tracking		
Other camera angles		
How many camera shots?		
Music		
Voiceover		
Other sounds		
Subtitles or inter-titles		
Transition to the next scene		
Key idea of this scene:		

be filmed out of sequence and reordered during editing. This can also lead to a discussion of continuity, i.e. when the position of props and the actors' clothes, hair, etc must remain the same, despite being filmed a number of times and at different angles, and so how to make a more professional finished product. It may be worth checking with the Drama or Media Studies/English departments in your school to see if they focus on film-making techniques and what their syllabus includes, as this may be a useful area for cross-curricular collaboration. There may also be film-making experts among the local community who could help launch the project.

Clearly this exercise would be best completed using a short piece of target language footage, perhaps from a film, published language teaching resource or from footage previously filmed with pupils. Demonstrating the key areas of film-making, rather than explaining them, enables more of the discussion to take place in the target language, and in Appendix 4 we include a list of film-making terms in French, German and Spanish to facilitate this. Nevertheless, as you are working with new concepts, and depending on the age and language level of the pupils, some of the discussion may be in English. In Chapter 4 we will look at more issues around use of the target language during the preparation, filming, editing and exploitation of a pupil-made digital film.

Pupils are likely to take the key messages of this exercise home with them and they may well watch *Eastenders* through new eyes! The relevance of such a lesson to the real world and of getting pupils talking about their MFL lessons at home, should not be underestimated.

The process of planning the filming has been seen to have benefits too for literacy and generic reading and writing skills. In a fascinating paper, *Moving images in the classroom*, David Parker, formerly of BFI Education, suggests a positive link between engagement with the moving image and the development of print literacy (both reading and writing), with a focus on primary pupils' understanding of narrative. Through working on a storyboard for an animated film based on a source text, pupils produced dialogues which featured, for example, a greater sense of context and setting, character point of view and causality of events, than those created by their peers who worked on a task solely in print. This equated to a development in literary practices, on average, of one National Curriculum level across the three-month project. It would be interesting to explore whether there is similar potential for pupils to express themselves with more clarity and coherence in their foreign language production as a result of digital video project work.

The second area of preparation for pupils is to establish what language the pupils can use in their film and where they can find support. It will help your role in monitoring the work of the groups of pupils if they are clear about how to work independently. Pinpointing the relevant language in the textbook, in pupils' exercise books and on vocabulary sheets will enable them to make progress with their scripts on their own. There is more advice on script writing in Chapter 4, however it is important to be clear with pupils why on-line translators and dictionaries need to be used carefully!

The third area of preparation for pupils is in working as a group, independently from the language teacher. Group work and encouraging discussion are not very common activities in language lessons and it is important to remember the benefits of working collaboratively:

> *Successful collaborative conversation can develop an individual's ability to think and reason in a way that is helpful when subsequently working alone. Effective group discussion thus provides children with the essential language tools for raised individual achievement.*
>
> (Littleton, Miell, and Faulkner 2004)

In the CILT/BBC 21CC research project several schools decided what roles would need to be filled so that all the members of the group were working equally.

Roles for film project

- The director
- The producer
- The director of photography
- The camera operator
- The actors
- The editor

The producer

- You are responsible for making a list of props and ensuring that the props are in the right place at the right time.

- You are responsible for checking that the locations you need are available. (You can overrule the director on this one!)

- You are responsible for managing the time available and getting people to move on.

This allocation of roles may be too prescriptive for some projects in which the pupils have more freedom in deciding on the type of film they are going to plan, but it is important to ensure that all the pupils in a group are included in the project in some way. As we can see from the example above it is not necessary for all pupils to be filmed; they can work the camera, be responsible for the props, direct the action, be the prompter, hold up the prompt boards, take charge of the editing, etc. What can be helpful is for each group to have a director or arbiter who can make final decisions if there is a need to settle a dispute. In some of the projects carried out in the CILT/BBC 21CC research, teachers found that pupils also worked well by each taking a role–filming, acting, directing and editing.

However, for some pupils, working collaboratively does not always come naturally, and problems within groups sharing ideas or making decisions can severely damage the final product as well as the pupils' motivation to complete the project. Establishing ground rules for working together is one way to prepare the pupils for working properly as a group, as well as looking ahead to what potential problems may arise while working together.

> The 'ground rules for talk' operate in the same way as rules for sport or a
> board game. They reduce the degrees of freedom of individuals in a way
> that ensures that the whole group can benefit from joint enterprise [...]
> While learning to collaborate, children can be made aware that there will
> be differences between their ideas, conclusions, theories, information,
> perspectives, opinions and preferences, which they can usefully state and
> rationalise. So, while everyone may offer competing ideas, intellectual
> development depends on co-operation with one another to examine these
> ideas and make meaning of one another's claims [...] Children are engaged
> with the subject of the discussion in a way that reduces the drive to comment
> on, or react to, one another's personal manner.

(Littleton, Miell, and Faulkner 2004)

Below is a list of rules that could be a useful starting point, however it is also good practice to ask the pupils to negotiate their own set of rules and express them in their language. In this way pupils have a sense of 'owning' the agreed ground rules.

Ground rules for group work

🎥 We will share all relevant information with each other.

🎥 We will ask everyone to say what they think and give reasons.

🎥 Everyone should listen to each other.

🎥 We will think about what to do together.

🎥 We will make sure that everyone is encouraged to speak.

🎥 We will decide what to do only when everyone has said all they want.

🎥 We will all try to reach an agreement.

🎥 We will all take responsibility for the decisions we have made and for the completion of the project.

How you divide the class into groups can also have a major influence on the outcome of the projects. In the CILT/BBC 21CC research project, several schools allowed pupils to choose their own groups as they considered that friendship groups would communicate and collaborate more effectively. However this is not an appropriate way of working with all groups or classes and you may need to take into account other factors, such as the size of the class, the ability range, the gender mix, personalities and behaviour profile. You may also want to take account of the pupils' creativity and ability to lead and collaborate, when deciding on the pupils who will work together.

In the latter stages of the project the groups' ability to collaborate may be included in the assessment of the outcomes, either as peer or self-assessment.

To conclude, one of the teachers who took part in the Becta DV pilot commented: 'using DV technologies provides a context and motivation for effective teamwork and communication, in which pupils were prepared to ignore personal differences in order to achieve a successful finished project'.

Key points

- A digital video project has benefits for pupils in their linguistic development, their ICT skills and in their ability to work in groups.

- In the preparation, filming and editing of the film, pupils are practising, developing and refining their knowledge of the target language.

- A film-making project can be included in a scheme of work or can form the basis of extra-curricular activities.

- It is essential to be up to date about current guidelines for filming pupils and to be aware of the relevant health and safety issues in the filming process.

- Film projects give you and the pupils the opportunity to explore a range of film genres and programme types.

- In order to carry out the digital video project, pupils need to know more about the process of filming and how to work effectively in groups.

Chapter 4
» Facilitating pupil-centred projects

- How can I support pupil planning and the generation of ideas?

- How can I structure the project around a series of lessons?

- What support will pupils need with script-writing?

- What are a storyboard and a shot list?

- To what extent can I expect the target language to be used?

How can I support pupil planning and the generation of ideas?

As you start to plan a film-making project you will have in mind how much direction you will give the pupils during the planning process. There are various levels to the direction you can give, as the following points show:

1 You give the pupils a completely free hand and allow them to decide on the type of film they will make and the language they will use. If this is the case then you may still need to set certain parameters for pupils, such as ensuring the inclusion of all members of the group, the length of the footage filmed, the location for filming, the target audience and the duration of the whole process, including how the film will be edited. This approach gives the pupils lots of scope for creativity and ownership of the project; it can also inspire pupils to produce highly original films. A danger however is that pupils attempt to use a lot of complex language, from dictionaries, on-line translators or from the foreign language assistant, and that they struggle to use and pronounce it correctly.

2 You begin with a brainstorm with the whole class around a particular theme or language area (see example opposite). For example, if the digital video project is part of a scheme of work you could suggest how pupils can use the language from a particular topic and combine it with already learned items. From that point on the pupils can make their own decisions about how their films will develop.

3 You give the pupils the context and language area, and they plan the film around these specific demands, using phrases and structures that you have provided. See *La maison hanteé* script-writing kit on p64–66 developed by Shireland College.

The points that pupils need to consider in the initial stages are:
• The overall aim of the project, e.g. creativity, pronunciation.
• The focus of the film, in terms of language and context.
• The audience and final use of the film.
• What technology will be used and how it will be accessed.
• If the films will be assessed and how.
• The duration of the project.
• The timescale for the different stages of the project, i.e. how many lessons or how much time for planning, filming and editing.
• The maximum length of the film and the footage recorded; ten minutes filming to achieve about one minute of film gives the pupils enough scope to develop their film ideas without having too much footage to edit.
• Whether roles need to be allocated or whether all pupils are to have a turn in each role.

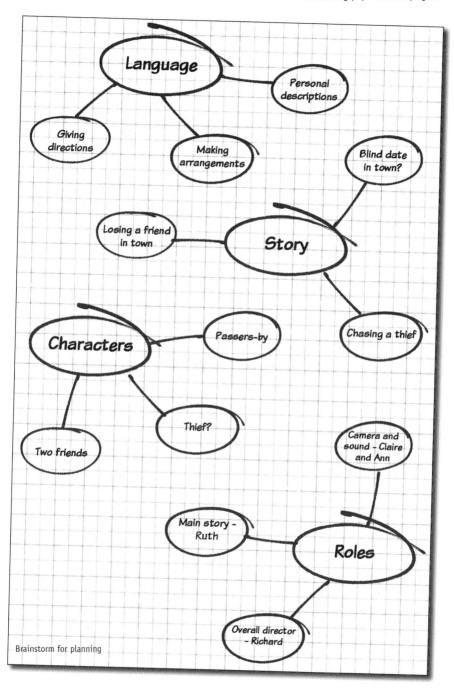

Brainstorm for planning

Year 8 Digital Video Project *La maison hantée*

SCRIPT WRITING KIT

Look at the French sentences in each section, and copy and paste the ones (only the French sentences) you want to insert in your film script.

<u>Do not cut and paste</u> as you may need the same sentence twice.

Some sections may not correspond to your scenes.

Saying 'hello' and introducing yourself	
Good morning, Sir/Madam.	*Bonjour Monsieur/Madame.*
I am Mr/Mrs ...	*Je suis Monsieur/Madame ...*
Is the house for sale?	*La maison est à vendre?*
I am the owner of the house.	*Je suis le propriétaire (de la maison).*
I live here.	*J'habite ici.*
I am from the agency '...'.	*Je suis de l'agence '...'.*

Visiting the house	
I would like ...	*Je voudrais ...*
I would like ...	*J'aimerais ...*
... to visit the house.	*... visiter la maison.*
... to see the house.	*... voir la maison.*
Please, enter.	*S'il vous plaît, entrez.*
There are ... rooms.	*Il y a ... pièces.*
Here is the ... (+ room).	*Voici le/la... (+ room).*
Do you like it?	*Vous l'aimez?*

Wanting to buy the house	
I love it!	*Je l'adore!*
I'll buy it!	*Je l'achète!*
Sold!	*Vendue!*

Seeing a ghost/monster ... and being afraid or not afraid!	
What is it?	Qu'est-ce que c'est?
Aaahhh! Help!	Aaahhh! Au secours!
How horrific!	Quelle horreur!
It is horrible!	C'est horrible!
I am scared (of ...)!	J'ai peur (des ...)!
There is a ... (+monster) in the ... (+room)!	Il y a un/une/des ... (+monster(s)) dans le/la ... (+room)!
There was a ... !	Il y avait un/une ... !
I saw a ... !	J'ai vu un/une ... !
He/She was... !	Il/Elle était ... !
... nasty!	... méchant(e)!
... horrible!	... horrible!
... terrifying!	... terrifiant(e)!
... amusing!	... amusant(e)!
The ghost/monster ... speaks!	
Leave!	Partez!
Leave my house!	Quittez ma maison!
Who is there?	Qui est là!
Mortals!	Mortels!
There are intruders!	Il y a des intrus!
... in my house!	... dans ma maison!
It is **my** house!	C'est **ma** maison!
Not believing you saw a ghost ...	
The house is not haunted!	La maison n'est pas hantée!
It is impossible!	C'est impossible!
It is an invention!	C'est une invention!

There are no ... (+ monsters).	*Il n'y a pas de ... (+ monsters)*
You are inventing this!	the agent speaking → *Vous inventez!* the friend speaking → *Tu inventes!*
Relax!	*Relax!*
Finding a solution	
I have an idea!	*J'ai une idée!*
Look!	*Regarde!*
It is simple!	*C'est simple!*
Be careful!	*Fais attention!*
Good luck!	*Bonne chance!*
The ending (either happy or sad)	
Hip hip hip, Hurray!	*Hourra!*
It is my house!	*C'est ma maison!*
At last, I am alone!	*Enfin, je suis seul(e)!*
Aaahhh ... It is over!	*Aaahhh ... c'est fini!*
Bye, intruders/strangers/mortals.	*Au revoir, intrus/étrangers/mortels.*
Aaahhh ... it is quiet now!	*Aaahhh ... c'est calme maintenant!*
Bravo!	*Bravo!*
Bye, bye house!	*Au revoir, la maison!*

Source: Shireland Language College

How can I structure the project around a series of lessons?

Timing the film-making project carefully will ensure that the pupils stay motivated and on task and also that they do not spend too long on any one of the different stages. You may find that they have very high expectations of the kind of film they can make and the standard of the final product, and it will be necessary to manage what they expect to achieve. For pupils who wish to continue refining their work they could be encouraged to do this out of lessons as it can be extremely time-consuming! This could offer an opportunity for pupils to gain credits through taking responsibility for refining a group film from the basic edit achieved in the lesson to a professional edit in homework time. A language teacher, foreign language assistant or other teacher could supervise a group working voluntarily after school. It may also be possible for the editing to be carried out in ICT, DT or Media Studies lessons. The editing process could be achieved in various ways:

- The pupils take it in turns using a small number of stand-alone laptops in the classroom.
- The pupils take it in turns using stand-alone computers in the ICT room.
- The pupils use networked computers in the ICT room, depending on the capacity of the network and the computers.
- The teacher edits the films.
- A small group of pupils volunteers to complete or finish off the editing in their lunchtimes or after school.
- Certain pupils edit their films at home.

How you manage your time with the pupils will depend on your access to technology, i.e. how many cameras you have and where and when your pupils can carry out the editing. It may be helpful to organise the lessons as a carousel so that groups take turns filming and editing, rather than having all the pupils doing the same thing at the same time. This work could be spread over a number of weeks, with small groups of pupils using one or two language lessons for editing. You may also find that making use of a small number of laptops in the languages classroom can be more effective than taking the whole group of pupils to the ICT room at once.

DV made simple

Carousel lesson

A lesson in which pupils work in groups and move around from one task to another. They are given time limits and work independently in the groups, with the teacher monitoring each group's progress.

In the CILT/BBC 21CC project several teachers commented that they needed to keep pupils to a tight schedule, as they can spend hours perfecting their scripts and do not realise how long they will need to film and edit the films. Knowing the overall schedule helped the pupils to see how quickly they had to work. Some schools put together booklets for the pupils to work through, so that they could develop their projects at different speeds and keep all their work in one place.

Nevertheless, there may be times when filming cannot happen or certain groups of pupils finish before the others. In the CILT/BBC 21CC project teachers at Tile Hill Wood School asked pupils to keep a reflective diary during the project and used any spare time to allow pupils to complete their diaries and to feedback from them to the rest of the group. In several other schools pupils also found time to complete an out-takes section which they then included in the final credits of their film.

DV made simple

Out-takes

These are scenes that were not in the original release of the movie. These scenes can be extra footage of a scene that was not used or when the actors or crew have made mistakes, either accidentally or deliberately.

To help ensure pupils complete their projects to a timescale, the plan for a series of lessons or tasks could look like this:

Task/Lesson	Activity
1	Analysis of film as example of different shots, filming techniques, etc. Brainstorm topic
2	Split into groups and discuss effective group work ground rules, discuss film focus, write overview of script, discuss/assign roles, work on script together in the target language. (At this stage it is helpful to have a script 'manager' who keeps the script safe, brings it to class, makes copies etc.)
3	More time for script-writing in groups.
4	More time for script-writing in groups plus homework to finish it.
5	Discussion of storyboard and shot list (see p70). Pupils complete these based on their scripts.
6	Rehearsing scripts, learning to use the camera and start of filming for some groups.
7 and 8	Rehearsing, filming in groups (completing 'self-access' worksheets if necessary).
9	Capture films, and select and order rough clips.
10 and 11	Editing the rough clips and adding music etc.
12	Showing and assessing the final films.

What support will pupils need with script-writing?

In the CILT/BBC 21CC research project the most successful films kept to language that pupils were familiar with, although the context for the language used was often highly original. This helped the pupils make their acting and use of the target language more confident, and also made the films more useful for presentation to other pupils. However, because the images themselves also convey meaning, pupils could be allowed to tackle more complex language if they really want to. Equally, a lot can be communicated with very little language in a film. The most important factor is that pupils are clear about what they are saying and can give their lines the correct delivery. It may help to plan an outline in English first, so that pupils are clear about what they are trying to achieve. However, as previously stated, it is important pupils avoid translating complex sentences and keep their expectations realistic.

What are a storyboard and a shot list?

One of the films made as part of the training for the CILT/BBC 21CC research project, was *La búsqueda*. The following pages describe the process of filming and show how to construct a storyboard, shotlist and script.

Storyboard

A storyboard is a visual representation of how each part of the film will look. It is like a list of the shots that will be filmed, but it is in chronological order. The storyboard can be completed at the same time as the script, so that the pupils are thinking about the visuals which will support the spoken lines. It will also help the group share ideas for how they want the scenes to look and to provide a skeleton of the story for editing later on.

The example for the storyboard structure for the film *La búsqueda* (see p73) includes lots of information about each shot or scene and this can provide a good starting point for pupils' planning. It assumes that the pupils will film in the order given. It is worth reminding pupils, however, that they may need to flexible with the plan, as ideas will occur to them as they film. For example in the CILT/BBC 21CC research project, several teachers found that their pupils did not plan for reaction shots or for changing from filming one person to another while filming a dialogue.

For an example of a storyboard go to 'The filming of *La búsqueda*', one of the films that was made as part of the training for the CILT/BBC 21CC research project.

Shot list

A shot list comes after the storyboard and scripting. It helps pupils both to consider the chronology of the film and to see if they can rearrange the filming in order to avoid problems with continuity. It consists of all the shots that will take place in a particular setting. Compiling a shot list is a complicated process and it may be that pupils will find it more logical and a lot easier to carry out their filming in chronological order, especially if the filming is taking place over a series of lessons. With more experienced film-makers or with a more complex storyline, a shot list is extremely helpful and will move the pupils on with their film-making skills. (See p75 for the shot list for the film *La búsqueda*.)

Camera skills

Pupils will need some training in using the school digital video camera, and will need to keep in mind the guidelines for film-making and health and safety that were covered in Chapters 2 and 3.

A simple list of things to check before filming could look like the following:

Filming checklist

✔ Check that everyone in the group knows what they are doing.

✔ Rehearse the script again and write on large sheets if necessary.

✔ Check the props and costumes.

✔ Check that the battery is charged and make sure you have a spare battery plus the microphone and clapperboard, if you are using them.

✔ Check that the prompter and director have the script, storyboard and shot list.

✔ Be careful with the wires you are using, don't trip!

✔ Watch out where you are filming, especially if it is outside, for noise and hazards such as cars, pavements and members of the public!

✔ Keep filming, don't rewind to see what has been filmed as this wastes the battery.

✔ The director or clapperboard operator should count down from five before filming: five, four out loud, and then 3, 2, 1 on his or her fingers.

✔ The actors should hold their positions for five seconds before the camera starts and after the filming has stopped, to allow for smooth editing.

✔ Try not to sweep the camera across the scene (panning) and don't zoom in. Reshoot the scene in close up.

✔ Be flexible with your script, as you may have some better ideas during filming. Use your time efficiently – you can edit the film later so that it is in the correct order.

The filming of *La búsqueda*

'We were given a short time to make a one-minute film in a foreign language. Our process started with an idea for the film which was to focus on personal descriptions in Spanish. We considered the setting that we could use and decided to make it a search around the local streets. We also had limited props and costumes and so decided to denote the passers-by in our film by giving them odd hats to wear.

We then put together a storyboard based on our script and attempted to include all the main shots we would use. This helped us work out a shot list so that we could be as efficient as possible with our time, filming each person saying their parts of the dialogues in the correct locations. These would then be put into the correct order during editing.

We practised the dialogue before going out to film and then scouted around for a location with not too much background noise.

During the filming we made various discoveries about our planning. We needed to have more establishing shots in order to give the overall idea about where the characters were. It was also quite tricky to have two people in the shot when we were filming dialogues. It made more sense to focus on one person for the whole dialogue, and then film the other person saying their part of the dialogue. This avoided having to move the camera too much between speakers, which can make the viewer a bit dizzy when they watch. We also didn't think enough about shots which come at the end of the dialogue; either we would need to film a reaction to the dialogue or to film each person saying 'Goodbye' or 'Thanks'. These shots helped to round off the dialogue neatly. So we had to be fairly flexible with the shooting as we were learning things as we went.

However it was important not to be too flexible with the script: too many changes would make editing more complicated, as it would be more difficult to identify which bits of the rough footage we wanted to use. We also did not allow very much time to practise the script and this meant that we spent more time having to refilm, because our acting needed more work! We realised later that we needed to be careful with the microphone; it was crucial to hold it as near as possible to the actors but without it getting into the shot!

With ten minutes of footage we edited our film to be about two minutes long. It took us longer than the other groups as we had included so many different scenes in our story and wanted to achieve certain effects. It was quite a surprise to us that it took so many shots to make a short section of film and for a simple story to be communicated, and we basically had too much footage! Where some of the action was not clear we added titles to the shot, as well as an opening title and 'The end' and credits at the end. We also put a music track over the film which became louder during the transitions from one scene to another and when there was no speaking. The filming took about an hour and the editing took around two and a half hours as the learning curve in this part of the project was much steeper for us.'

Participant in CILT/BBC 21CC project

Section of storyboard for *La búsqueda*

Scene 1

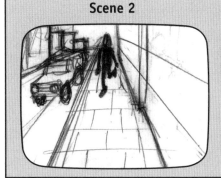

Camera use:
Ann filming. Medium close up of Richard.

What is happening:
Richard is looking at his watch and is angry. He walks out of camera.

What is being said:
¡Ay, ay, ay! ¡Qué tarde es!
¿Dónde está Ruth?

Sounds/Effects/Subtitles:
Music goes up at the end of the scene.

Scene 2

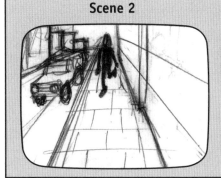

Camera use:
Ruth filming. Long shot of Ann.

What is happening:
Ann is walking down the street.
She is wearing a funny hat and smiling.

What is being said:

_____

_____

Sounds/Effects/Subtitles:
Music carries on loud.

Scene 3

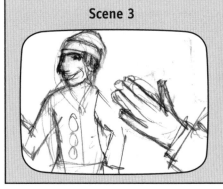

Camera use:
Ruth filming.

What is happening:
Ann is walking down the street and Richard stops her by putting his arm out.

What is being said:
¡Por favor!

Sounds/Effects/Subtitles:
Music fades out at the start.

Scene 4

Camera use:
Ruth filming. Only Richard is in shot

What is happening:
Richard is asking about his friend and describes her.

What is being said:
¿Ha visto a mi amiga? Es rubia y baja.

Sounds/Effects/Subtitles:

Scene 5

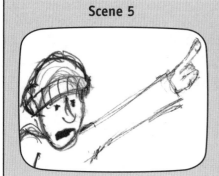

Camera use:
Ruth filming. Only Ann is in shot.

What is happening:
Ann is answering the question.

What is being said:
Sí, sí. Se fue para allá.

Sounds/Effects/Subtitles:

Scene 6

Camera use:
Ruth filming. Only Richard is in shot.

What is happening:
Richard thanks Ann.

What is being said:
Gracias.

Sounds/Effects/Subtitles:

Scene 7	Camera use:

Camera use:
Ruth filming. Close up on Ann.

What is happening:
Ann is laughing.

What is being said:

_____

_____

Sounds/Effects/Subtitles:
Music comes back loudly.

Shotlist for *La búsqueda*

Shots 1 to 3 Richard

Shot 1 = Richard looking at watch. (Scene 1)
Shot 2 = He describes his friend. (Scene 4)
Shot 3 = He says thanks. (Scene 6)

Shots 4 to 7 Ann

Shot 4 = Ann walking down street. (Scene 2)
Shot 5 = Ann walking down street and Richard stops her. (Scene 3)
Shot 6 = Ann tells Richard the direction his friend went. (Scene 5)
Shot 7 = Ann reacts by laughing. (Scene 7)

Shot 1   Shot 2   Shot 3   Shot 4

Shot 5   Shot 6   Shot 7

Outline story and roles for *La búsqueda*

Roles

Principal director: Ann
Principal camera operator: Richard
Principal sound operator: Claire
Responsible for script and story: Ruth

Props

Two silly hats

Setting

A pavement in town

Overall story

Two friends arrange to meet back at one o'clock when they are out in town. But they miss each other. They both go off looking for each other and ask passers-by if they have seen their friend. They describe their friend but the passers-by deliberately give them the wrong information. At the end they run into each other and the passers-by laugh about how mean they have been.

Section of script for *La búsqueda*

(Richard arrives. Looks at watch.)

Richard: *¡Ay, ay, ay! qué tarde es! ¿Dónde está Ruth?*

(Ann comes down street. Richard stops her.)

Richard: *Por favor ¿Ha visto a mi amiga? Es rubia y baja.*

Ann: *Sí, sí. Se fue para allá.* (Ann points away.)

Richard: *Gracias.*

(Ann laughs hysterically as Richard walks away.)

In English: The Search

Richard: *Oh, oh, oh, look how late it is! Where is Ruth?*

Richard: *Excuse me. Have you seen my friend? She is blonde and short.*

Ann: *Oh yes. She went that way.*

Richard: *Thank you.*

To what extent can I expect the target language to be used?

Making use of the target language in a different context is one of the principle motivations behind teachers wanting to organise a film-making project. As we have seen, however, there is a good deal of technical explanation and organising that will need to happen before and during the film-making process. You will need to have in mind which set of instructions or explanations can be carried out in the target language, and which in English, to make the project run smoothly but also with maximum benefit for the pupils' use and understanding of the target language. This is 'incidental' use of the target language and it can run alongside the actual target language script.

In the CILT/BBC 21CC project many of the schools found that there was some scope for using the target language for certain parts of the process, but they also admitted that with the technical side of the project, e.g. health and safety guidelines for filming, use of the camera and the editing of the films, they needed to use English to be clear about the messages they were giving.

The amount of 'incidental' target language can increase as the pupils become more experienced in filming and as they become more advanced language learners. If the target language is not used throughout the film-making process this is not a reason to abandon the idea of a film project. The pupils' use of the target language can be woven into the process and, with some planning by the teacher, pupils will come to know certain processes only by what they are in the target language.

The parts of the process where 'incidental' target language could be used are:
• brainstorming ideas for the film;
• guidance for script-writing and storyboarding;
• naming different shots and film terminology, for example when analysing a piece of target language film, as in Chapter 2 (see Appendix 4);
• using the target language terminology in the storyboard and shotlist;
• using instructions while rehearsing and filming (see Appendix 4);
• writing parts of the script onto large sheets of paper behind the camera, if pupils need support with their lines;
• naming the different parts and functions of the camera;
• naming the different clips or sequences while capturing the film during editing;
• in the titles, inter-titles and sub-titles added to the film footage;
• in the assessment criteria for pupils or the teacher to use.

Key points

- Pupils can sometimes need more help in structuring their plans for a film than may at first be apparent. However working within certain constraints, like language or location, can increase their creativity.

- When you are planning the timing of a project you need to include how the editing process will take place, as this will have a big influence on how long the pupils can spend on the preparation and filming stages.

- You will need to check the pupils' scripts before filming starts and decide how tolerant to be of errors they may have made, bearing in mind that they will be practising the scripts and committing them to film.

- Writing a storyboard based on their script gives the pupils an opportunity to write in a new medium.

- During the film-making process pupils will need lots of support to use the target language. It can be most useful for instructions, e.g. Cut! Places!, and for labelling the roles and the different stages of the process.

Conclusion

With the rapid advances in technology available to teachers we need to keep in mind how that technology can support good practice in language teaching. We want our pupils to be confident in their language skills and to be able, in some way, to perform in the foreign language. It is our belief that film-making in languages lessons supports many of the aims we have for our pupils.

In simple 'point and shoot' activities, pupils are adding value to what they are doing already and making immediate use of their language skills in a variety of creative ways, and they have the opportunity to reflect on their language skills and improve on them. In larger projects pupils plan, write, rehearse, perform and listen to the foreign language, and, above all, have the opportunity to make it their own.

The films produced can bring more variety to your assessment practice and provide models for pupils or other teachers to respond to. The final films can be an expression of the pupils' identity and interests and allow some personalisation of the learning in their languages lessons.

At certain stages of film-making it may be the case that discussion is not focussed on the language but about the way the camera works, what kind of shot to include or how to use the editing software. However, for pupils, the benefits of completing their own film are enormous: motivation increases, they practise their language skills, they collaborate in groups, they act, direct and extend their ICT skills. Moreover, they create an original piece of work. As one of our *Digital Video in the MFL Classroom* project schools said: 'The sense of satisfaction in producing an 'artefact' in the target language is considerable' (Torquay Boys Grammar).

There are further ways to make an impact with your final films and to share and celebrate your pupils' achievements, as exemplified by the CILT/BBC 21CC project schools. Some films were used as 'Welcome' videos for school foyers; some were shared with partner schools in other countries; others were used in assemblies and parents' meetings or with local primary schools. Films were entered for education competitions and some schools held awards ceremonies of their own, rewarding acting and technical skills, as well as language use. One school even had the idea of 'film trailers' being the focus of a project, so that the trailers could then be used for a mock film awards ceremony. Many schools made sure that pupils taking part in the films had their own copy on CD-rom to keep.

As with using many types of technology, we have to start somewhere and we hope that the first two chapters of the book have given you the confidence to go ahead with filming and editing, and to think of contexts for filming pupils and ways of making effective use of your films for teaching and learning. Chapters 3 and 4 will have given you ideas for some longer film-making projects, allowing pupils to take over elements of the process and exploring how the project can be embedded within a scheme of work. Many of the Digital Video in the MFL Classroom project schools pointed out that it was desirable for all members of the languages department to learn film-making skills, especially if all pupils were to have equal access to the skills and if schemes of work were to be used in common. Some of the teachers were also approached by other departments to share skills or equipment and it is clear that there are opportunities here for cross-curricular collaboration, either in the area of professional development or in setting up projects between languages and other curriculum areas.

The range of films that can be produced in languages lessons is as varied as the pupils or teachers making them. We hope that we have stimulated your imagination and provided support here for whatever kind of film maker you are and the kind of film you aim to produce.

Appendix 1
» Selecting an appropriate format for saving video files

DV format offers the best quality, but this requires a lot of storage space. Other, more compressed file formats, may be more appropriate for your needs. If you save video clips as .avi, .wmv or.mpeg/mpeg2/mpeg4, for example, the files will be of manageable size and should play through Windows Media Player on your computer. You can also insert such files into PowerPoint presentations, for example, integrating the clips into your teaching resources.

Be aware that your computer will need what is known as the correct **codec** to play a video file. Making sure you have the most recent version of Windows Media Player installed will usually ensure you have the correct codec. Where you have an older version of Windows which does not support the most recent Player version, you can usually download **plug-in** software from the Microsoft website. If you are working on a Mac computer, you are more likely to be using the QuickTime player, which can handle most video formats. Do consult your network manager on these issues!

DV made simple

Codec
A standard technology for compressing and decompressing data, particularly video and audio, to reduce file sizes. It is short for compressor-decompressor. An operating system or a program (e.g. your media player) uses a codec, for example, to decompress video to play it back on the computer screen. A popular codec for computer video is MPEG.

DV and mini-DV format
DV is a very commonly used video format which uses tape cassettes. Mini-DV tapes (and cameras) are usually smaller than other DV tapes.

Plug-in
A piece of software that plugs into a main software application to give it added capability. Plug-ins are very often free and downloadable from the Internet.

A standard DVD player plugged into your television will not necessarily be able to play digital video files saved from your computer onto a disk, whether a (re)writeable CD or DVD. A DVD in this context is simply a data storage CD with much greater capacity. Where there is the facility on your DVD player to play back digital video files, those in .mpeg/mpeg2/mpeg4 format will usually play, as long as the disk was 'closed' correctly. Such a DVD can be opened and played on a computer with a DVD ROM drive.

There is also the option of creating a DVD using DVD authoring software on your computer, such as Power DVD, Nero or Roxio. Authoring software allows you, for example, to create a menu of options with background music as on a commercial DVD, resulting in a more professional-looking product. Such a DVD can be played on a standard DVD player and on a computer with a DVD ROM drive.

Appendix 2
» Guidance for parent permission letter for filming pupils

Guidance for obtaining permission from parents for filming may vary in different contexts and in different local authorities. We have therefore put together some ideas of what you might include in a permission letter to send to parents.

Firstly, check that the school has not contacted parents as a matter of course to secure parental permission for filming activities. You will need to clarify if any pupils do not have permission and the limitations of the permission, particularly in terms of dissemination.

Your letter could include:
• a summary of the project, including the start and end dates;
• plans for dissemination;
• sanctions if pupils misbehave (linking to home-school contract);
• educational aims;
• why permission is sought.

You may also want to add paragraphs which cover the following points:

1 What the school will do to ensure the safety of pupils:
• The risks of using digital video with pupils are minimal however the school has a duty of care towards pupils and recognises that it needs to ensure the welfare and safety of all young people (see Appendix 3, p87).
• The school will not permit video or other images of young people to be taken without the prior consent of the parents/carers and children.
• The school will take the necessary measures to ensure that the images are used solely for the purposes for which they are intended.
• At no point will the images of the pupils be linked to their full names.
• Any breaches of the code of behaviour by pupils will be dealt with by the appropriate school sanction.

2 How the images will be used:
- The images may be used as teaching resources within the curriculum, in display around the schools and on the internal school website.
- The video clips may be used as teaching aids within the curriculum and for staff training and educational purposes at both local and national level.
- At no time will the images be sold or made available for wider publication, such as on the school's public website, without further parental approval.
- The school will ensure that the images are only available for use by the pupils involved in the project.

3 How the images will be stored:
- The images will be stored securely in the MFL Department and will be kept for no longer than two years.
- The images may be stored in the form of CD ROMs or on the school computer hard drive and access to the images will be monitored by the teachers in charge of the digital video project.

4 How the pupils will be supervised during filming:
- The school will ensure that pupils are properly supervised in the school while filming and will inform pupils about the health and safety tips for filming.
- If any filming is to be carried out outside the school grounds, separate permission will be sought.

You may also want to add a form that can be returned to you, such as the following:

Please complete, sign and return this form to:

....

....

Name of child:

....

....

Name of parent or carer:

....

....

Address:

....

....

....

....

....

I have read and understood all of the above and I agree that my child can take part in the project using digital video:

....

We have read and understood the 'Safety tips for digital video projects' that the school will abide by:

....

Signature: .... Date: ....

Queries regarding this form should be addressed to:

....

....

....

Appendix 3
» Safety tips for digital video projects

✔ Do run leads along the wall, rather than across the floor, if at all possible.

✔ Do use 'gaffer tape' or duct tape to hold cables down safely.

✔ Do be careful if you're using film lighting: stands can fall over, bulbs can burst, things can get very hot. If you have to bring in lights, make sure you know how to use them safely.

✔ Do make sure that when using lighting, any safety glass or guards are in place.

✔ Do be careful to check the sound level on headphones to avoid damaging pupils' hearing.

✔ Do remember to turn down the volume, or disconnect the audio cables, when your camera is connected to a monitor in camera mode: audio feedback can be very loud.

✔ Do remember to turn down the volume on amplifiers and/or headphones before connecting or disconnecting any equipment.

✔ Do get parental permissions before embarking on a project. You'll need to think about issues of safety in terms of using pupil images, as well as parental permissions for external field trip activities. See the 'Safety issues' section on the Becta CD-ROM *Teaching and learning using digital video* for more information about pupil images and a template of a parental consent form which you can download and adapt.

✗ Don't let people bang microphones or connect and disconnect cables while pupils are wearing headphones.

✗ Don't touch or move hot lights – wait until they've cooled down.

✗ Don't run mains cables out of doors or where they might get wet.

✗ Don't run mains cables through doorways or windows where they might get crushed.

✗ Don't concentrate so hard on filming that you're not aware of what's going on around you. Be careful of tripping over if you're walking with the camera.

✗ Don't film with anything dangerous behind you – it's easy to forget and step backwards. (This includes steep drops, stairs, roads, rivers and fires.)

✗ Don't walk backwards with your eye to the viewfinder unless you have somebody guiding you.

Source: Becta website **http://schools.Becta.org.uk**

Appendix 4
» Film-making terminology

General terms

English	French	German	Spanish
Digital video	la vidéo numérique	das digital Video	el vídeo digital
Script	le script	das Drehbuch (ü +er)	el guión
Storyboard	le scénario	das Storyboard	el guión gráfico
Dialogue	le dialogue	der Dialog (e)	el diálogo
Lines	(apprendre son) texte	der Text (er hat seinen Text vergessen)	el papel
Video camera	la caméra	die Videokamera (s)	la videocámara
Cassette	la cassette	die Kassette (n)	el casete
Props	les accessoires (m)	die Requisiten	el atrezzo
Set	le décor	der Drehort/das Set	escenario
Costumes	les costumes (m)	das Kostüm, die Kostüme	el vestuario/los trajes
Make up	le maquillage	die Maske	El maquillaje
Lighting	la lumière	die Beleuchtung/das Licht	la iluminación/las luces
Sound	le son	der Ton (ö +e)	el sonido
Microphone	le microphone	das Mikrofon (e)	el micrófono
Record/Pause/Stop button	le bouton pour enregistrer/pause/arrêt	die Aufnahmetaste/ Pausetaste/Stopptaste	el botón para grabar/ pausa/stop
Voiceover	une voix-off	das Voice-over	la voz en off
Backing track	la bande sonore	die Hintergrundmusik	la banda sonora
Sub-titles	les sous-titres	der Untertitel ()	los subtítulos
To dub	doubler	synchronisieren	doblar
Dubbing	le doublage	die Synchronisation (en)	el doblaje
Film clip	le clip	der Filmclip(s)/ der Filmausschnitt (e)	el vídeo clip

Verbs/Instructions

English	French	German	Spanish
Lights, camera, action!	Lumière, caméra, ça tourne!	Licht, Kamera läuft, Los!/ Licht, Kamera läuft, Action!	¡Luces, cámaras, acción!
Cut!	Coupez!	Schnitt!	¡Cortad!
Freeze!	Arrêtez!	Stop!	¡Parad!
Record	Enregistrer	aufnehmen	grabar
Delete	Effacer	löschen	borrar
Edit	Éditer	Bearbeiten/überarbeiten	editar
The recording/take	La prise (elle est bonne! = it's a take!)	die Aufnahme (n)	La toma

Roles

English	French	German	Spanish
Director	le réalisateur	der Regisseur(e)/ die Regisseurin (nen)	el director/la directora
Camera operator	le cameraman	der Kameramann/ die Kamerafrau	la cámara
Actor	un acteur	der Schauspieler()	el actor
Actress	une actrice	die Schauspielerin (nen)	la actriz
Cast	la distribution/les acteurs	die Schauspieler/ die Besetzung	el elenco/el reparto
Extras	les figurants	die Statisten	los extras
Editor	un éditeur	der Herausgeber()/ die Herausgeberin (nen)	el editor
Sound engineer	un ingénieur du son	der Toningenieur(e)/ die Toningenieurin (nen)	el ingeniero de sonido

Camera shots

English	French	German	Spanish
Zoom	le zoom (zoomer)	das Zoomobjectiv(e) heranzoomen/wegzoomen	el zoom/acercar/alargar con zoom
Pan/Scan	faire un panoramique	der Kameraschwenk/ schwenken	rodar una (vista) panorámica
Close-up	un gros plan	die Großaufnahme (n)	un primer plano
Long/Wide shot	un plan long/un plan large	die Totale	un plano grande/ una toma larga
Cutaway shot	un plan de coupe	der Schnappschuss (ü +e)	unl plano de corte
Angle	un angle	der Winkel	el ángulo
Fade out	faire disparaître en fondu	ausblenden/ die Ausblendung	esfumar/fundir a negro

» References

Becta (2002) *Teaching and learning using digital video* (CD-ROM). Becta Publications.

Becta (2004) *Digital alchemy: Using digital video assets across the curriculum* (CD-ROM). Becta Publications.

Burn, A., Parker, D. and Reid, M. (2002) *Evaluation Report of the Becta Digital Video Pilot Project*. BFI Education.
www.becta.org.uk/page_documents/research/dvreport_241002.pdf

Burden, K. and Kuechel, T. (2004) *Evaluation report of the Teaching and Learning with Digital Video Assets Pilot 2003–2004*. Becta Publications.
www.becta.org.uk/page_documents/research/evaluation_dv_assets03.pdf

Dawes, L. and Sams, C. (2004) 'Developing the capacity to collaborate'. In Littleton, K., Miell, D., and Faulkner, D. (ed) *Learning to collaborate: Collaborating to learn*. Nova Publishers.

DfES (1990) *Modern Foreign Languages for ages 11 to 16*. DfES.

DfES (2003) *Excellence and enjoyment: A strategy for primary schools*. DfES.

Hawkins, E. (1987) *Modern Languages in the Curriculum*. CUP.

Littleton, K., Miell, D. and Faulkner, D. (eds). (2004) *Learning to collaborate: Collaborating to learn*. Nova Science Publishers Inc.

Parker, D. (1999) *Moving images in the classroom*. BFI Education.
www.bfi.org.uk/education/research/teachlearn/nate.html

Websites

Audacity – **http://audacity.sourceforge.net**

Becta Schools – **http://schools.becta.org.uk**

Becta Publications – **http://publications.becta.org.uk**

British Film Institute – **www.bfi.org.uk**

Digital Video in Education – **www.dvined.org.uk**

Flash Kit – **www.flashkit.com**

Media Education Wales – **www.mediaedwales.org.uk**

Notre Dame High School – **www.ndhs.org.uk**

UK Intellectual Property Office – **www.ipo.gov.uk**